人間冥煙

For Heaven's Sake

人間冥煙

香港紙紮文化

For Heaven's Sake

Hong Kong's Paper Offerings for the Afterlife

高峰 著

Chris Gaul

香港中文大學出版社

The Chinese University of Hong Kong Press

《人間冥煙：香港紙紮文化》

高峰 著及攝影
陳曉蕾、高峰 譯

國際統一書號：978-988-237-282-5

2022 年第一版
2023 年第二次印刷

出版：香港中文大學出版社
　　　香港 新界 沙田・香港中文大學
　　　傳真：+852 2603 7355
　　　電郵：cup@cuhk.edu.hk
　　　網址：cup.cuhk.edu.hk

香港印製

特別感謝：
帕特・阿姆斯壯、陳麗珊、陳萃忻、
陳穎華 、 張惠笙、何書佩、洪茜昵、
郭斯恆、伊芙・蘭德、李慧嫻、
艾璐思、蕭競聰、楊可郡、張琳傑

For Heaven's Sake: Hong Kong's
Paper Offerings for the Afterlife

Text and Photography by Chris Gaul
Translated by Yoyo Chan and Chris Gaul
Copyedited by Phoebe Rapp

ISBN: 978-988-237-282-5

First edition 2022
Second printing 2023

Published by:
The Chinese University of Hong Kong Press
The Chinese University of Hong Kong
Sha Tin, N.T., Hong Kong
Fax: +852 2603 7355
Email: cup@cuhk.edu.hk
Website: cup.cuhk.edu.hk

Printed in Hong Kong

With special thanks to Pat Armstrong,
Mary Chan, Sui-Yan Chan Kristy, Wing
Chan, Alice Hui-Sheng Chang, Supei Ho,
Chien-Ni Hung, Brian Kwok, Eve Lande,
Rosanna Li Wei-Han, Eloise Rapp, King-
Chung Siu, Kay Yang and Linjie Zhang

目錄 Contents

序言 蕭競聰
Foreword King-Chung Siu — vi

自序
Preface — xvi

寄託在紙紮中的香港人情
Offerings of Devotion: Hong Kong in Paper — 2

紙紮品照片集
Photographs of Paper Offerings — 36

點只衣紙咁簡單 李慧嫻
Paper Offerings Have Much More to Offer
Rosanna Li Wei-Han — 180

詞彙表
Glossary — 199

冥府產品和服務供應商
Underworld Product and Service Providers — 200

照片索引
Index of Photographs — 202

Foreword

King-Chung Siu

Chair, Community Museum Project

What makes Hong Kong's paper offerings for the afterlife so fascinating? Perhaps it's that they are a form of material culture that is at once both whimsical and worldly. As art educators say, paper offerings are not only a folk craft but also a contemporary artform that reflects the richness of human imagination and experience. Though they are focused on the dead, paper offerings reflect so much about human life. Just as when choosing gifts for friends and family, you must always give careful consideration to the tastes, temperaments, and needs of others. This way, you can make smart and meaningful purchases that express your love and sincerity.

Chinese society puts great importance on familial relations, and Chinese people are meticulous about putting this into practice through festive meals, weekend tea gatherings, mahjong sessions, and seasonal gifts. Keeping up with relatives and friends in the afterlife is no different. Traditional funerals are elaborate ceremonies that express and reflect the thoughts of the deceased through the language of the material world. Each year at Qingming, Yu Lan, and Double Ninth festivals, the residents of this world connect with those of the next. Families gather together to burn paper offerings,

序言

蕭競聰

「民間博物館計劃」主席

　　為什麼我們都對香港的紙紮祭品及其文化著迷？我想，大概由於它是人類物質文化中一組既異想天開、又非常「世故」的類型。一如藝術教育家們所說的，它不單可以像當代藝術般表現出當地的傳統技藝、反映生活，以至於開發種種人文想像，而且充滿人情世故──只不過是以先人為主要對象而已。就如選贈禮物給親朋好友，你總要充分考量他人的喜好、性情和需要，以作精明而有意義的消費決定，來表達你的情誼和誠意。

　　華人社會重視人倫，實踐方式極其細緻。親朋戚友總會找方法，比如透過喜慶宴客、週末茶聚、攻打四方城、時節送禮等，去維持良好的人際關係。對逝去的先輩、親屬和友人也不例外，大家不忘設計精細的悼念儀式，以物質世界的「語言」去表達和體現對亡者的思念。傳統喪禮之外，每年的清明節、盂蘭節、重陽節等等，也都是陽間

incense, and candles, and make offerings of food, fruit, and flowers. Giving paper offerings is a way to commune with the departed. The practice reflects care and creativity towards ancestors while revealing the materialistic imagination of the Chinese world.

Of course, to show proper respect, the living should never be sloppy or skimpy when buying paper offerings for deceased relatives and friends. If your father enjoyed dim sum at the teahouse, you should be sure to send him some Iron Goddess tea, chicken feet, and shrimp dumplings. For a late mother who loved mahjong, a good son or daughter should arrange a set of tiles and a gaming table—even some players to join her. And why not send a big bowl of *poon choi* for them to share? If your relatives are into fashion and accessories, you can find 'Cartire', 'Channel', 'Gugi', 'LX', 'Pierre Cardier', 'Rolax', and 'Patik Philipe'. There are even bicycles, skateboards, record players, and game consoles to keep young departed spirits entertained. In the afterlife, everyone can hold a home return permit or a passport—even hundreds of millions of dollars—to cross to mainland China or travel the world. And they can carry a high-resolution camera or the latest 'ePhone' to post photos from their trip. For something more daring, you could even order a luxury car, private jet, or yacht to let your loved ones chart their own course. In their travels, they may encounter some dizziness, nausea, vomiting, or stomach pain. But as long as you prepare a paper travel medicine bag with Albino oil, Po Chai pills, Centipede tablets, and other familiar local remedies, there won't be a problem!

Our care and concern for relatives and friends is truly fastidious. Financial stress, depression, or longings for the finer things should not exist in paradise. We show our respect and commitment to our family by ensuring that they have whatever they need to lead a carefree eternal life.

與陰間大眾聯誼的日子。陽人親友聚首一堂，以香燭、花果、餐用祭品、紙紮禮物等跟先人神交，喃喃自身的願望和抱負。饋贈紙紮禮品體現了我們對先人的心意和創意，更說明了華人世界的物慾想像。

要為先人選購禮物，陽間親友當然不應馬虎：亡父喜歡嘆茶、一盅兩件，於是就找來紙紮鐵罐音、鳳爪和蝦餃；亡母喜歡湊腳打麻將，於是準備好紙紮麻將和麻雀枱，有需要更可訂製紙紮雀友，確保亡母九泉之下都不愁沒有玩伴，耍樂完畢還可以一齊吃頓盆菜；你甚至可送贈紙紮寵物狗或紙籠相思雀給親友解悶。若家人喜歡名牌服飾、手袋、手飾等潮流名物，什麼 Cartire、Channel、Gugi、LX、Pierre Cardier、Rolax、Patik Philipe⋯⋯應有盡有。針對年輕亡魂，也不乏有益身心的玩物，如單車、滑板、唱機、遊戲機⋯⋯確保祂們在陰間生活充實愉快。在冥界，大家更可持回鄉證和國際護照，甚至億萬金元，縱橫中國大陸、周遊列國；更可配備高解像相機或最新款 ePhone 打卡拍照。豪爽一些的，可訂購紙紮房車、私人飛機或遊艇，讓你的摯愛縱橫四海。路上頭暈身熱、疴嘔肚痛，只要帶備旅行藥包，裏頭有白化油、保劑丸、蜈松散等特效成藥問題就不大了！

我們對陰間親友的關懷和眷顧，可謂無微不至，為生計煩惱、苦悶、缺乏細藝等一切生活困擾都不應存在於極樂世界的清單上。陽人對先人的尊重和承諾，就是要確保大家豐衣足食、要乜有乜、永恆的生活無憂。

As you can imagine, where there is demand, there is supply—along with mechanisms and networks for design, production, and marketing. If we Chinese or Hong Kong people had not lost sight of our filial values, Hong Kong's paper offering shops may not be in such a state of decline. But, in this era of ever changing technology and online consumption, perhaps these networks could manifest in new ways. Rosanna Li Wei-Han was part of the exhibition *Supermarket of the Dead* in Germany, which imagined a new business model for paper offerings: being able to shop for them at large paper offering supermarkets. When Rosanna and I chatted, we even dreamed up local convenience stores where you could pick up items for ancestors—just like stopping in at the 7-Eleven. In such a world, this book, *For Heaven's Sake*, could be a kind of shopping guide. In it, you'll find all the goods and daily necessities your loved ones may need in the afterlife.

From traditional clan rituals to the material culture of our technological era, the Chinese vision of the afterlife has changed dramatically. Traditional moral virtues of loyalty, filial piety, propriety, and righteousness are no longer abstract and difficult to understand—affection and care can now be expressed by giving tangible gifts. By purchasing paper offerings, you can stimulate economic consumption while continuously satisfying your consumer desires (and justifying this as paying respect to your ancestors).

Although the traditional papercraft masters are retiring, a new generation of 'paper offering product designers' are taking their place. For example, my friend Au Yeung Ping-Chi has created a range of contemporary made-to-order offerings,[1] including stormtrooper helmets from the film *Star Wars*. From the sci-fi world of cinema, to real-world craft creations, to 'spiritual commodities' in the next world—Hong Kong's next generation are showing a far-reaching spirit of innovation that can't be ignored!

可以想像，有需求就有供應，就有設計生產和行銷的機制和網絡。如果我們（華人或香港人）的人倫價值沒有丟淡，香港的紙紮衣紙店鋪也許不會式微；而在時移世易的科網消費世代，更大有可能以改頭換面的方式存在。李慧嫻在德國參與的《冥間超市》展覽，預視了新穎的紙紮生意模式：每逢白事、清明和周年悼念或祭祀的日子，陽人可在各家紙紮超級市場為先人選購生活用品，以表情意和思念。我們閒談時更想像過，將來若有像7-Eleven般的社區小店，專營銷售紙紮生活商品，也未嘗不可。反正這就是為冥界而設的禮品店，由陽人世世代代地營運。《人間冥煙》這本小書就像一份購物指南，你大可在裏頭找到各類貨種和閣下親友在陰間所需的日用品。

從物質文化和現今科技世代的角度去思考，我們想像的極樂世界，跟傳統宗族禮教所描繪和體現的道德倫理已有不少轉變；那些有關忠、孝、禮、義的倫理不再抽象難明，大家都可透過饋贈有形的禮品來表達情義與關懷。大家透過選購禮品，一同刺激消費，促進經濟循環；透過饋贈禮品，以永續滿足自身的購物慾望。為他人（或先人）購物的那份情意，可平衡一下自身購物慾所附帶的自私感。

儘管紙紮師傅退休老去，新一代的「紙紮商品設計師」會以全新姿態出現。例如友人歐陽秉志[1]就創製了不少當代的紙紮系列讓客人訂購，包括電影《星球大戰》中的黑、白兵頭盔。從電影中的科幻創意，到陽間實質的工藝

Contemporary designers, in addition to designing for the living, might also consider designing products for the afterlife. Providing a kind of 'designer lifestyle' for the ancestors could be said to be the ultimate way of paying respects. British artist Damien Hirst recently offered works at an auction where buyers were asked to choose between the physical artwork and its NFT (Non-Fungible Token—a kind of digital file). If the buyer opted for the NFT, the physical work would be burned.[2] Were I the buyer, I would have no hesitation in choosing the NFT. So long as the piece that Hirst burned went through some festive rituals, it could be sent to the afterlife for my late father to add to his collection. He loved art and culture, so why not add a contemporary masterpiece to his house to demonstrate his son's devotion?

Our consideration for our ancestors' afterlives is parallelled in the current AI generation's imagination of the so-called metaverse. We are all concerned that our ancestors enjoy a perfect afterlife, and we naturally attend to their clothing, food, shelter, food, drink, and entertainment. The living create various products to meet the needs of the dead. Where there is a product, there is a market; where there is a market, there is consumption; and, where there is consumption, the economy can be developed. In a way, it forms an industrial and economic structure that combines the *yin* of the afterlife with the *yang* of this world. It is probably not difficult for the tech world to find inspiration for the construction of the metaverse in this marketplace of paper.

I recommend this book to technologists building the metaverse. Paper offerings provide source material and reference tools for a virtual network of things, complete with social, political, and economic dimensions. There are banks and currencies in the afterlife; housing and even real estate; designer jewellery and clothing; Visa cards, Octopus cards, private cars, luggage, and passports.

創作，再到開發冥界「精神商品」的想像，處處都體現了香港新一代無遠弗屆的創新潛質，真不容忽視！

所有設計師，除了為市民大眾設計生活必需品外，也可同時參與設計陰間的生活商品，為先人設計祂們合意的生活方式，可謂體現人倫關係的極致。近期英國藝術家 Damien Hirst 把自己的作品複製成 NFTs（非同質化代幣，一種新型的數位檔案）後拍賣，並要求買家只可在實體和虛擬作品兩者選其一：若買家選擇收藏 NFT 版本，他就會把作品燒掉。²若我是買家，我會毫不猶疑地收藏 NFT，因為 Hirst 燒掉的那件作品──假如經過一些節日祭祀儀式──可以送往冥界給先父收藏。先父也是愛好藝術文化的一輩，何不為祂的陰宅添一件當代名家作品，以表兒子的孝道？

我們關顧先人摯愛在陰間的生活起居，跟現時 AI 世代對「元宇宙」的想像，實有異曲同工之處。大家關心冥界的極樂生活，就自然想到先人衣食住行、吃喝玩樂的情況，陽界就可為冥界設計和生產各類產品，以滿足需求。有產品就有市場，有市場就有消費，有消費就能帶動經濟，形成陰陽兩界結合的產業和經濟結構。科技界正在進行中之元宇宙基建，大概不難從這個紙紮市場得到啟發。

我建議建造元宇宙的科技人員參考此書，因為這些紙紮品，為元宇宙世代提供了虛擬極樂世界的生活素材和工具參照，揭示冥界（甚至元宇宙）生活的物聯網，以至其

There are regions and national boundaries, commodities and transactions. There is entertainment and socialising, perhaps even roads and infrastructure. In the years to come, the metaverse will surely become as rich and diverse.

In this perfect world, everyone can forget the troubles of work and life; when there's work to be done, it can be taken care of without lifting a finger. This is the essence of paper offering culture, strengthening the bond between the living and the dead. Let this book be your guide.

July 2022

1. Siu Hiu-wah, 'Baohua Zazuo zi cheng fu ye chuantong yu xinchao zazuo yishou baoban,' 〈寶華扎作子承父業傳統與新潮紮作一手包辦〉 *Ming Pao Weekly (Culture)*《明周・文化》 May 15th, 2018.

2. Eileen Kinsella, 'Burn, Baby, Burn! Damien Hirst Will Set His Own Drawings Aflame in the Culmination of His Grand NFT Experiment "The Currency"', artnet.com, July 26, 2022, https://news.artnet.com/market/damien-hirst-burning-art-2152134.

社會、經濟和政治面貌：陰間有銀行和貨幣；有住屋甚至房產；有名牌首飾和衣履；出門有Visa咭、八達通、私家車、行李喼和護照等等；有地域和國界；有商品有交易；有玩樂有交際，也許都有道路和基建——衣食住行兼娛樂無窮。來年元宇宙虛擬網絡的世界，想必也將會那麼多姿多彩。

在這個極樂世界，大家都忘卻工作和生活的煩惱；即使有工作要處理，也不用費舉手之勞，能被好好地照顧著。這正是紙紮文化暨過節燒衣、陰陽聯誼派對吸引之處。本書可給大家一個導覽。

2022 年 7 月

.

1. 蕭曉華，〈寶華扎作子承父業傳統與新潮紮作一手包辦〉，《明周・文化》，2018 年 5 月 15 日。

2. Eileen Kinsella, 'Burn, Baby, Burn! Damien Hirst Will Set His Own Drawings Aflame in the Culmination of His Grand NFT Experiment "The Currency"', artnet.com, July 26, 2022, https://news.artnet.com/market/damien-hirst-burning-art-2152134.

Preface

Hong Kong is a captivating city, and one that I've been lucky enough to visit many times. One of my favourite things to do there is to walk through different neighbourhoods, experiencing the energy and rhythms of everyday life. On one of these walks, I came across a bustling papercraft workshop. Workers were busy constructing paper models of luxurious houses, and the workroom was filled with paper replicas of barbecued ducks, aeroplanes, and small people with bright pink faces. This was the first time I'd seen people making paper offerings for the dead. I was fascinated by these charming models and curious about their significance in people's lives.

A few years later, finding myself at a loose end, I decided to return to Hong Kong to explore this world of paper offerings with more purpose. Before setting off, I reached out to an expert: King-Chung Siu, a researcher and lover of Hong Kong's everyday design culture. King invited me to meet him at his office at the Polytechnic University and, after chatting for some time, he suggested we take a walk to nearby Hung Hom, the city's funeral district. We saw people working on the footpath, deftly fashioning large-scale paper offerings. We browsed some of the small shops that sell the types of offerings featured in this book. Though the trade is said to be in its sunset years, I was surprised and excited to see a vibrant craft industry surviving into the twenty-first century.

自序

　　香港是個令人著迷的城市。我多次到訪，尤其喜歡到不同地區散步，感受都市日常的活力和節奏。有次走著走著，經過一間熙來攘往的紙紮工場，看到師傅們忙著製作紙紮豪宅，店內則堆滿各式紙祭品，如燒鴨、飛機、皮膚鮮粉紅色的人偶等。那是我第一次看到師傅即場紮作供奉先人的紙祭品，而深深被他們的精巧手藝所吸引，想多了解它們對生命的意義。

　　數年後，我閒著沒事，決定重回香港，進一步探索這個紮作世界。涉足前，我向一直熱中研究香港日常設計文化的蕭競聰請教。我們在他的理工大學辦公室見面，略談一會後，他便建議一起到附近的紅磡區走走，看看這個殯儀業的集中地。行人路上，有師傅熟練地製作大型紙紮。我們又逛了數家包羅萬有的小店，本書亦有涵蓋它們出售的種類。雖然有人視紮作為夕陽工藝，但看到這個行業在二十一世紀仍然屹立不倒，令我非常驚喜。

　　及後五載，我每年都有幸回到香港，教一個關於本地設計文化的短期大學課程。教學以外，我走訪城中大大小小的紙號。在新界，小販檔在墓地外的公路上一字排開，

Over the next five years, I was lucky enough to return to Hong Kong each year to teach a short university course about the city's design culture. Between teaching commitments, I spent my time exploring paper offering shops across the city. In the New Territories I found hawker stalls lining the roads to cemeteries, selling offerings for families to burn at the graves of loved ones and ancestors. On Hong Kong Island, I visited the impressive shops on Queens Road West. Some of these stores were big enough that their offerings were arranged in sections, almost like a department store. Sadly the biggest of these have recently disappeared and are being replaced by luxury apartments. I worked my way across Kowloon, visiting smaller neighbourhood stores where customers and staff were always busy chatting. I was so curious to know what they were talking about and wished I could strike up a conversation, but I only knew the most basic Cantonese.

Language wasn't my only limitation. I was also restricted by a modest budget and the dimensions of Hong Kong Post's largest carton box. There were so many offerings I would have loved to collect—I always came away from the paper offering shop wishing for more. I had to walk away from life-size electric guitars coated in red glitter, bicycles, cooktops with attached gas bottles, fancy dogs with curly paper rolls of fur. Perhaps these longings reveal something of my own preferences for the afterlife. In any case, however many I collected, I could never match the vast range of products on offer. Within these limits, I set about curating the selection that appears in this book. My hope is that it will give you a sense of what Hong Kong offers for the afterlife. Most are staple items (dim sum dishes, wardrobe essentials, household items and the like) but some reflect trends in the paper offerings market at the time (sushi, streetwear, and tech goods, among others). I have aimed to show a range of designs—some simple, others creative or unusual—and I've taken a particular interest in offerings that are unique to Hong Kong.

一間我在上環路經的紙號，於拍下這相片的數年後結業

The paper offerings workshop I came across in Sheung Wan.
It closed a few years after this photo was taken.

The makers of the works featured in this book are unknown to me. These days, paper offerings are only occasionally custom made by well-known masters. Like most of the offerings for sale, the objects photographed for this book were handcrafted according to a pattern. Usually, I would find a few of the same object for sale in a store, especially for popular offerings like clothing and food. Sometimes I found the same design in different stores and, occasionally, I found a one-of-a-kind; possibly the last of its type to be sold.

After picking out and purchasing a selection of offerings in a shop, the staff would bundle them into suitcase-sized red plastic shopping bags for me. Loaded up with this fragile cargo, I negotiated the city's crowded streets, narrow turnstiles, and busy buses, trams and trains. With one load safely stashed in my room, I would head out again in search of the next. By the end of each visit to Hong Kong, my tiny room would be overflowing with paper objects. Before leaving for the airport I carefully wrapped, boxed, and posted them. A few days later, a stream of paper offerings would start arriving at my home in Australia, almost as if I had arrived in the afterlife. I stored them in my house (to the concern of some of my Chinese friends' parents, who felt this was liable to bring me bad fortune) and photographed them in a makeshift home studio.

In photographing these objects, I've aimed to showcase their ingenious and creative designs and to draw attention to their most interesting features. Smaller paper offerings are usually sold and burned in decorated protective paper boxes. In some cases, I've photographed offerings without their boxes so that they are easier to see. Sometimes I've taken an item out of a boxed set and photographed it separately to draw attention to it. I've included multiple photographs of objects that move. You'll likely recognise most of the objects, but if you want to know what they are, you can find short descriptions in the index at the back of the book.

售賣各款紙祭品，供家屬燒給祖先或至親。在香港島，皇后大道西的紙號令人一見難忘，有些較大的店鋪如同百貨商店般分門別類地展示各式紙紮。可惜，這些大型紙號近年已絕跡，取而代之的是奢華簇新的住宅樓宇。我又踏遍整個九龍，參觀了不同地區的老店。店內總見到顧客和店員「雞啄唔斷」，似有說不完的話。我很好奇他們在談什麼，亦很想和他們聊天，無奈我只懂得最基本的廣東話。

語言障礙以外，我還遇上其他挑戰，包括經費緊絀，以及香港郵政的萬用箱的尺寸限制。紙號總有一股魅力，吸引我不斷回訪尋寶。但面對云云相當值得珍藏的紙祭品，我不得不作出取捨，像是忍痛放棄如實物般大小的紅色閃爍電結他，還有單車、連石油氣罐的煮食爐、用波浪紙條裝飾的鬈毛犬。這些渴求，或也反映了我對身後事的喜好。但無論如何，即使我的收藏再多再廣，也只是紮作世界的冰山一角。本書的選材受以上因素所限，但我希望它能呈現香港對來生的想像與關顧。除了點心、衣物、家品等生活必需品，紮作師傅亦會緊貼當下潮流，推出壽司、街頭服飾、科技產品等祭品。本書望能展示紮作設計的多樣性，有較簡潔常見的，也有富有特色、充滿創意的，而我對香港獨有的紙紮品，特別感興趣。

本書收錄的眾多紙祭品，均不知出自何人之手。近年市面上的紙紮，甚少是由大師個別設計和訂造；市面上買到的，亦即本書收錄的，多為按式樣製作的現成品。店內

To give context to the photographs, I've written 'Offerings of Devotion: Hong Kong in Paper'. In this short introduction, I've outlined how paper offerings are constructed, sold, and burned, and shared some thoughts about the custom's significance and future. I hope this text can familiarise readers who are new to the culture and reacquaint those who have grown up with it.

Being an outsider to Hong Kong and its world of paper offerings comes with obvious limitations. I would love to more easily make connections with people, learn about their lives, and listen to their stories. But being in this position has its benefits, too. Learning about a culture from an outside perspective allows you to see its customs with a fresh pair of eyes. When I would tell people from Hong Kong that I wanted to make a book about paper offerings for the dead, the usual response was a short pause followed by a puzzled 'Why?' Some wondered why I would needlessly bring such a large helping of bad luck on myself. But most seemed surprised that I would take such an interest in something so everyday and unremarkable.

When media attention is given to paper offerings, it is often focused on the latest outrageous or extreme designs. It's not surprising then that many outsiders think the custom is silly and unsophisticated. Certainly there are amusing and, from time to time, even distasteful designs. But a remarkable aspect of paper offering culture is its ability to reflect everything about life, from the absurd to the ordinary. Offerings can be preposterous or poignant, heartwarming or heartbreaking. Each worshipper can choose an offering that reflects their relationship with the recipient.

I'm fortunate to be able to complement my outsider's view with those of two expert insiders. King-Chung Siu has kindly written the foreword to this book. King has been researching and shaping Hong Kong's art and design culture for over thirty years. He is a

多放著數個同款紙品，當中衣物和食品尤其暢銷。我常在不同店鋪看到設計一模一樣的紙品並列，但有時也會找到獨一無二、大抵是售完即止的孤品。

每次選購紙紮後，店員都會用大如行李箱的紅色膠袋包裝。我就帶著這些吹彈可破的工藝品，穿梭大街小巷，擠進巴士、電車，與地鐵上的乘客大眼望小眼。每次我回到住所安放心頭好後，總按捺不住再出發尋寶。離港前，小小的房間總是擠滿紙品，我每次赴機場前也要忙著小心逐一包裹入箱，再郵寄到澳洲。數天後，一捆又一捆的紙祭品陸續抵家，猶如我已到達來世。我把它們存放家中（有些華人朋友的父母擔心我因此會交上厄運），在陋室搭建的攝影棚拍照。

為這些紙品拍硬照時，我希望能捕捉它們原創破格的設計，凸顯個別的有趣特色。小型紙品多放在精美的紙盒發售和燃燒。我有時會先取出才拍照，有時更會逐一拍攝套裝內每個細物，以便更清晰呈現。本書亦包括一些有機關的紙品。大部分的紮作均清晰可辨，但如有興趣了解更多，請見書後索引的簡短介紹。

為補充背景，圖輯前的文章〈寄託在紙紮中的香港人情〉簡介了紮作技藝的文化，概述紙祭品的製作、售賣和焚燒過程。我亦分享了對紮作的角色和未來發展的一些想法，除了讓更多人了解這個文化外，本地人也能重溫它的魅力。

co-founder of the Community Museum Project and has written several excellent books, including *Lesser Designs* and *Designs You Don't Know What to Do With*. In 2019, King introduced me to his friend and colleague Rosanna Li Wei-Han. Rosanna is one of Hong Kong's most respected ceramicists. If you are in Hong Kong, you can see some of her much-loved sculptures at Yau Tong MTR station. She is a witty and playful artist and designer who has been fascinated by paper offerings since her childhood growing up in Hung Hom. She has kindly written a wonderful essay for this book, which follows the photographs.

After spending several years learning about the custom, I've come to see paper offering culture as a touching and thoughtful expression of human relationships. Paper offerings are a way to care for others—sometimes in surprising ways. Among the offerings I found is a beat-up black and gold boombox. I was surprised it was for sale: it was bent out of shape and most of its dials were about to fall off. The seller was offering it at a discount, but I'm not sure who would want to make an offering of it. I liked it enough to buy it, but, being so badly damaged, I didn't bother to photograph it and instead put it away in a box. Several years later, I took it out and noticed something hidden inside. I cut through the sticky tape that held the cassette deck closed and, to my surprise, found a paper cassette (it appears on page 177). The label on the cassette says that it is a recording of *The Flower Princess*, a famous Chinese opera, performed by the Underworld Opera Troupe (one of dozens of underworld companies, departments, and organisations featured on the offerings found in this book. You can find a full list of them at the back of the book). I was amazed that someone has taken the time to craft this cassette, for a customer who will never know it is there, so that it can be offered to a listener in another world.

我作為香港的外來者，研究這個城市及其紮作世界時，當然面對不少限制。我很想更輕易與這兒的人連結，了解他們的生活，聆聽他們的故事。不過，置身這種處境也有好處，就是從外了解一種文化時，可以嶄新目光檢視傳統習俗的種種。每當我告訴香港的朋友，打算寫一本關於紙紮祭品的書時，他們常頓一頓，然後露出滿頭問號的樣子。有些人疑惑為何我要自招不必要的厄運，更多人好奇我為何對此不起眼的日常事物感興趣。

　　有關紙紮祭品的傳媒報道，多聚焦在標奇立異的新設計，因而令很多外來者誤會，以為這是個無聊、甚至幼稚的習俗。有些設計的確引人發笑，間或甚至不堪入目，但紮作這個文化，著實能反映生活中每個荒謬或平凡的細節。不論祭品看起來是可笑或深刻，窩心還是傷感，每位祭祀者均可透過選擇紙紮，表達自己與逝者的關係。

　　我有幸得到兩位專家的幫忙，為我這外行人的看法提供補充。為本書撰序的蕭競聰，過去三十多年來一直研究和影響香港的藝術和設計文化。作為民間博物館計劃的創辦人之一，蕭競聰曾出版多本精彩著作，包括《捹西設計》和《唔知做乜嘅設計》。2019年，他介紹了朋友兼同事李慧嫻給我認識。她是香港著名陶藝大師，最為人熟悉的雕塑作品為油塘地鐵站生色不少。這位風趣幽默的藝術家和設計師，因兒時在紅磡長大，自小已對紮作文化著迷。她應邀為本書撰文，收錄在圖輯之後。

One master said that he doesn't really believe that his paper crafts end up in heaven. And yet he has dedicated his life to making them so as to bring comfort to people who believe that they do. Making, selling, and burning paper offerings are acts of love and devotion. This book, itself a bundle of paper, is an offering to these makers, sellers, and burners. It is a record of their dedication and devotion and of their contribution to Hong Kong culture. Paper offerings spend only a short time in this world before they are sent to the next. My hope is that this book can allow a memory of them to linger here a little longer.

Chris Gaul
July 2022

研究這個習俗數年後，我愈發覺得紙紮文化細膩地表達了人與人之間的情感連結。紙祭品總流露著對人的關懷──有時甚至是以令人意想不到的方式。在眾多收藏品中，有一個黑金色的卡式機我在店內找到時已「甩皮甩骨」，整個變形，大部分按鍵幾近脫落，但出奇地仍在待售。雖然店家作特價發售，但我猜未必有人認為它適合拿來祭祖。儘管我把它買了下來，但因為太過破爛而懶得拍照，就直接入箱貯存。數年後拿出來看時才留意到盒內藏物，便剔開黏著磁帶卡座與主機的膠紙，驚訝地發現原來內藏著一餅卡式錄音帶（見第177頁）。磁帶上的貼紙寫著著名粵劇《帝女花》，由冥都劇團主唱（屬云云地府公司、部門、組織之一，詳見書後羅列的名單）。我很驚訝有人願意花時間製作了一盒連顧客都不知其存在的錄音帶，默默為另一個世界的聽眾帶來娛樂。

　　有位師傅直言，他不太相信自己的出品真的能送達天國，但他仍畢生致力紮作，希望能為相信的生者帶來一絲安慰。製作、出售、焚燒紙紮祭品均充滿著愛與奉獻。我僅以同為紙品的這本書，獻給所有師傅、紙號和祭祀者，望能記錄他們的用心付出，以及對香港文化的貢獻。紙紮祭品在送往來世前只在現世逗留片刻，我衷心希望本書能略為存續它們的印記。

高峰

2022 年 7 月

陰陽兩界只隔一層紙。

——俗語

The distance between this world and
the next is but a sheet of paper.
— Chinese folk saying

Offerings of Devotion:
Hong Kong in Paper

Wander the vibrant markets and shopping streets of Hong Kong's older neighbourhoods and you will discover a charming world of paper replicas of everyday items. These replicas are offerings to lost loved ones, and are destined for another world. According to Chinese custom, the dead can bring no belongings with them to the afterlife. Instead, they must rely on the living to provide for them by burning paper replicas of the things they want and need. As the paper withers to ashes and smoke, the offerings pass from this world to the next, where they take their genuine form.

Within this world of paper are offerings of every shape and kind, fit for every possible purpose. With so many designs and styles to choose from, worshippers can find just the right offerings for their loved ones. For a departed grandfather: a pair of slippers, some cigarettes and a songbird. For a beloved mother: a new purse, a favoured dim sum dish, and a portable radio to listen to Cantonese opera. For a former business partner: a gold watch, the latest digital organiser, a briefcase, and a new suit. For a daughter or grandson: a violin to practise, a new badminton racquet, study materials, and perhaps the latest video games. Individually, each offering

寄託在紙紮中的香港人情

在香港舊區漫步時，常見紙紮祭品出現於大街小巷。紙紮是後人給先人的祭品，供他們在另一個世界享用。據中國傳統習俗，逝者離開塵世時，帶不走任何財物，必須依靠後人燃燒各樣日常用品的紙紮，滿足他們在陰間的生活所需。隨著彩紙化作飛灰，祭品便會自陽間送到身處另一個國度的先人手中。

在紙紮的花花世界裏，製品的形態和種類五花八門，滿足各式各樣的要求。祭祀者總能從林林總總的設計和款式中找到最切合親人的祭品。仙遊的祖父或要一雙拖鞋、數根香煙和一隻了哥。摯愛的母親該會喜歡一個新錢包、一籠最愛吃的點心和一部便攜式收音機收聽粵劇。前生意夥伴能用上金錶、最新款電子手帳、公事包和新西裝。女兒或孫子會需要小提琴繼續練習，還有羽毛球拍、一些書本，以及最新電子遊戲機。每件祭品都代表著跨越陰陽的

represents an intimate and personal connection that transcends worlds. Collectively, they are a microcosm of Hong Kong that reflects the city's desires, obsessions and beliefs.

These paper offerings are made from colourful paper or card and held together with glue. Elaborate or irregularly shaped designs are made with a bamboo frame wrapped in crepe paper or papier mache. Fancier offerings feature cellophane, beads, metallic card or moulded plastic. Some boast moving parts: bags with functional zippers; umbrellas that open and close; desk fans with spinning blades and rotating heads; retractable fishing rods complete with functioning paper reels. Objects are typically life-size, though anything larger than a piano or a car will be modelled at a more convenient scale (without compromising its final size in the afterlife). Mass-produced designs are common nowadays, but the charming pieces constructed and decorated by hand remain popular. A few papercraft masters still fill custom orders for obscure fancies or exact reproductions of cherished possessions.

Worshipping supplies stores dotted across the city sell premade paper offerings for a modest price, and staff can advise on putting together appropriate and auspicious selections. These little shops also sell incense, ceramic deities, festival decorations and offering stoves. Hawker stalls in street markets and outside of cemeteries sell premade offerings as well. Stationery and variety stores sometimes stock a small selection of items for the dead, alongside products for the living. Funeral parlours offer large and lavish paper replicas to accompany funeral ceremonies.

Hong Kong's style of paper offerings are not like the precise, meticulous replicas made in Taiwan or the mass-produced offerings from Mainland China. On first impression, they appear cartoonish and simple. But, on closer inspection, it becomes clear that they are purposeful interpretations that capture the essence of the object

Above: The Mong Kok branch of Tin Chao Hong
Worshipping Supplies in Canton Road Street Market

Overleaf: Paper offerings outside the main store of Tin
Chao Hong on Queens Road West in Sai Wan. This was the
largest paper offerings store in Hong Kong until it recently
closed to make way for luxury shops and apartments.

上：廣東道街市天就行香燭紙業旺角分店

次頁：西灣皇后大道西天就行總店外的紙紮
品。 這裡曾是香港最大的紙紮品商店之一，
直到最近不敵名店和豪宅入侵，宣布歇業。

they are destined to become. Each replica emphasises the salient features or characteristics of the original, as judged by the maker. When these replicas are viewed as a whole, a revealing impression of Hong Kong comes into focus.

All these paper offerings, skilfully crafted as they may be, are destined to be tossed onto a fire. The ritual is not strict and is performed according to personal or family custom. Offerings are burned beside graves or on a neighbourhood street. They can be burned on the ground or in small stoves (the usual style is made from red enamelled metal with small air holes cut in the shape of stars or gourds). Temples and crematoriums provide decorated brick furnaces that accommodate large offerings. Small offerings are often bundled into a purpose-made offering bag. These colourful paper bags are embellished with floral patterns and holy messages and even come with an address label and afterlife postage stamps.

The ritual of burning paper offerings is intimately associated with three festivals: Ching Ming and Double Ninth festivals, when many families across Hong Kong make offerings to ancestors and tend to their graves; and the Hungry Ghost festival, when ghosts and spirits are said to wander the streets. Suppliers stock an abundance of offerings leading up to these festivals and sometimes put out a steel drum in front of the shop for burning offerings immediately. At Ching Ming and Double Ninth, paths to the city's cemeteries are thronged with hawkers selling premade offerings.

There is a fear among believers, particularly the elderly, of being forgotten in the afterlife. Those who have no relatives to make offerings for them may make arrangements with a paper seller to burn offerings on their behalf. Others who do not want to burden their families may do the same. Followers of traditional customs from Teochew (a city in nearby Canton) avoid this predicament entirely by selecting and burning items for themselves while they are alive in this world. But most rely on their family to take care of them.

親密牽絆。紙紮世界也是香港的縮影，反映了這個城市的嚮往、執迷和信念。

這些紙紮祭品由彩紙或卡紙製成，並以膠水固定組裝。繁複或不規則形狀的款式會先製竹框，再以在皺紋紙或紙漿包裹而成。較為精緻的紙紮祭品則用上玻璃紙、珠子、金屬卡片或模製塑料等材料。當中更不乏可活動部件，例如：帶功能性拉鏈的袋、可開合的雨傘、設轉動扇葉和旋轉頭的座枱式電風扇，以及配設紙捲軸的伸縮釣魚竿。紙製品多按物件的實際比例製作，然而體積大的物件如鋼琴或汽車則會按比例縮小，製成較輕便的模型（而到達冥界時仍會呈現本物的尺寸）。批量生產的紙紮祭品現今相當普遍，但人手製作的款式依然廣受歡迎。有些紙紮師傅仍會為客人量身訂造新潮的紙紮品，或完美複製先人生前的心愛物件。

常見的化寶爐
A typical stove for
burning paper offerings

紙號遍布各區街頭，以相宜的價格出售現成紙紮品，客人亦可尋求店員的建議，選購合適的祭品。這些小店還出售香燭、陶瓷神像、節日裝飾和爐灶。街頭市集和墓地外的小販攤位也會出售現成紙紮品，有些售賣生活用品的文具店和雜貨店亦有少量祭祀用品的存貨。殯儀館則提供大量較豪華的紙紮，以供陪葬。

油麻地謝全記紙號
Tse Chuen Kee Paper
Offerings in Yau Ma Tei

In the Chinese supernatural order, the veil separating the living and the dead can be lifted from both sides. The dead appear in dreams to make requests or complaints; it pays to keep them happy, as their curses or blessings can make trouble or bring luck. The living sometimes turn to divination to uncover the desires and needs of the departed. The most superstitious may consult mediums known as 'ask rice women', so named for the role of rice in their séances. (A spirit possessing the ask rice woman throws handfuls of rice to identify relatives.) In return for dutiful and lavish offerings, the dead will bestow blessings and good fortune. In turn, the living give shape and form to the afterlife with their choice of offerings.

香港的紙紮品，不如台灣製造的紙紮般精確細緻，又不像中國大陸批量生產的祭品。驟眼一看，簡約的製品或許充滿卡通感，但細察下，不難發現它們都刻意捕捉原物的神髓。每個紙複製品都按師傅的判斷，強調了原物的特徵。而這些複製品，還概括呈現了香港的深刻印象。

　　紙紮祭品，不論製作如何精巧，仍逃不過被扔到火裏燒毀的命運。焚燒儀式頗為隨意，大多根據個人或家庭習俗進行。祭品可在墳墓旁邊或城內的大街小巷上化灰，亦可席地在化寶爐燃燒（紅色琺瑯金屬製成，並帶有星星或葫蘆形狀氣孔的小型燒爐）。大型祭品可用寺廟和火葬場的金爐焚燒，小型祭品通常會被捆綁放在特製的附薦袋中。這些彩色紙袋多印有花卉圖案和福傳字句，甚至寫上地址和貼上冥界的郵票。

　　焚燒紙祭品的儀式與清明節、重陽節和孟蘭節這三個節日息息相關。每年的清明和重陽，不少家庭都會前往墳場掃墓，拜祭祖先。據說每逢孟蘭節，孤魂野鬼都會在街上閒逛。店家會在這些節日前準備豐富的祭品，有時還會在商店前面放置一個鐵桶，供人立即在街上燃燒紙祭品，亦即俗稱的「燒街衣」。在清明和重陽節期間，通向墓地的小路都會擠滿了販售現成紙紮的小販。

　　部分信眾，尤其長者，擔心離世後被遺忘。如沒有親友祭祀，或不願為家人帶來負擔，也可以委託店家代為燒毀祭品。潮州傳統習俗的信眾為了完全避免這種窘況，

Spirit money is the quintessential paper offering to the dead. Banknotes are styled after the U.S. or Hong Kong dollar or, more recently, Mainland China's *renminbi*. The prominence of banknotes among offerings reflects the significance of money in Chinese history and culture. Notes are issued by The Bank of Hell and bear the signature, seal and portrait of Yuk Wong, the mythical Jade Emperor. Yuk Wong regularly appears on offerings bound for the afterlife, depicted in a tasselled crown and imperial robes. These days, spirit money is available in ever higher denominations—million, billion and even trillion dollar notes—with no signs of the ruinous effects of hyperinflation. For those seeking more tangible investments there are gold and silver ingots made of foiled paper. The banks of the afterlife also issue cheque books, pass books and credit cards—all indispensable in a city obsessed with finance. Such offerings ensure the deceased can pay off debts to the spirits, buy their way into heaven, and make lavish purchases when they arrive.

Before departing for the spirit world, the recently deceased must ensure their papers are in order. The Chinese supernatural order resembles the social and political order of our own world. Yuk Wong sits atop a thriving bureaucracy that oversees every aspect of the afterlife. Consequently, all kinds of official documents are burned as offerings. Replica travel permits allow the deceased to enter the netherworld. Passports follow the format of their earthly equivalents, with personal details and pages for acquiring visas. Underworld versions of the Home Return Permit (the travel document used by Hong Kong residents when travelling to Mainland China) allow spirits to cross the border and return to their ancestral homes. Replicas of Hong Kong's Octopus card allow the dead to ride the mass transit of the spirit world. Coach, railway, and airline tickets facilitate the journey to heaven. (Some worshippers go so far as to offer a private jet, or even a small fleet of airliners.) Travel insurance

油麻地謝全記紙號外的大型遊艇

A large-scale yacht outside Tse Chuen
Kee paper offerings in Yau Ma Tei

甚至會於在世時自行挑選和焚燒祭品。不過，大多數還是付托家人料理後事。

　　陰陽兩界，只隔著一層紙，垂在先人與生者之間。逝者可入夢提出請求或投訴，而由於他們的詛咒或祝福可能會帶來麻煩或運氣，所以確保他們順心也能令生者安心。生者有時會通過占卜，了解逝者的心願和需要，較迷信的人更會諮詢人稱「問米婆」的靈媒（鬼魂顯靈附身於靈媒後，會扔出數把米以識別親戚）。為了能定期收取豐厚的供品，死者會祝福祭祀者好運，而生者亦從透過祭品的選擇，影響陰間的生態。

　　冥錢是最不可或缺的紙祭品。鈔票的款式多參照美元或港元的設計，近年亦有見人民幣。在云云紙紮中，層出疊見的冥錢反映了金錢在中國歷史文化中無可比擬的地位。紙錢由冥通銀行發行，印有玉皇大帝的簽名、印章和肖像。玉皇大帝頭戴冕冠、身穿龍袍的肖像亦常見於不同祭品。時至今日，冥錢的面額（數百萬，數十億甚至數萬億美元）遠超現實中鈔票的價值，但完全沒有惡性通貨膨脹的跡象。偏好實物資產的投資者，則可選擇錫箔紙製成的金銀錠。冥通銀行還發行了在這個金錢掛帥的城市中不可或缺的支票簿、存摺和信用卡。世道難行錢作馬，這些祭品令逝者可以還清神明的債務，死後也能安枕無憂。

　　前往冥界前，逝者必須準備好所有身分證明文件排列得井然有序。人間建立社會和政治結構以維持秩序，陰間

offers additional peace of mind on the journey. And, when the dead take up residence in the afterlife, driving licences, healthcare cards and gym memberships ensure access to the best facilities.

On arriving in the afterlife, the dead must have a place to live. Home ownership is a formidable challenge in Hong Kong and it's not surprising that paper offerings reflect a desire for housing stability. The city's housing market is among the most expensive in the world, and most people struggle to secure a place of their own. A lucky few live in luxury apartments, but thousands of the city's poorest live in 'coffin homes': cramped and dangerous subdivisions hardly bigger than a narrow single bed. Title deeds for the afterlife secure a home or even an enviable property portfolio in heaven. More often, the house itself is fashioned as an offering: villas or mansions—complete with pools, gardens and house keepers—are the most popular. The typical design is modelled on the two-storey villa found in Hong Kong's rural New Territories. High-rise flats, though much more common in Hong Kong, are almost never recreated as paper offerings. But at least one papercraft supplier sells crude replica coffin homes (a cheaper alternative to elaborate paper mansions for worshippers on a tight budget)—even the harsh realities of Hong Kong's housing market are faithfully reproduced for the afterlife.

Though the dead depart with nothing but the clothes on their backs, they can receive offerings of clothing in every style and for every occasion. Papercraft stores stock everything from traditional Chinese garments to modern street wear. And there are all kinds of shoes and accessories as well. Paper makers offer jewellery in traditional Chinese styles, imitating jade or gold, as well as modern, international styles. Reading glasses and sunglasses are popular offerings, as are handbags, watches and shoes. These clothes and accessories are some of the most intimate offerings. They ensure

旺角卓悅文具店。除了文具外，一些
文具店亦同時銷售供先人使用的紙紮
生活用品。

Cheuk Yuet Hong stationery store in Mong
Kok. This shop sells everyday items for the
living alongside paper offerings for the dead.

the deceased are protected and comfortable, and allow them to express their personal style in the next life.

When the basic needs of their loved ones have been met, worshippers' concerns turn to transportation for the afterlife. Luxury cars are a familiar sight on the streets of Hong Kong, and are a popular choice for paper offerings. The preferred offering is a classic British chauffeured saloon, though high-performance cars are a popular alternative. Life-size paper reproductions are sought after, but expensive. These cars are often finished with gold or silver foil and come with an auspicious number for the registration plates (which mimick the standard British-style Hong Kong plate format). Most sport the badge of a prestigious manufacturer and some boast a three-dimensional hood ornament, fashioned from foil. Much more affordable are the smaller mass-produced and imported replicas, which are about the size of a shoe box. At least one paper workshop produces custom orders for large-scale replicas of Hong Kong's lorries—the distinctive vehicles that carry live seafood, produce and other goods around the city.

Luxury yachts have become a common offering. Like cars, they can be bought at large and small scale. The harbour of the after-life is plied by fishing boats, sampans, barges and container ships custom-made by local paper workshops. Hong Kong is defined by its harbour, so naturally maritime workings are reflected in the city's paper offerings.

Eating is at the heart of life in Hong Kong, where food is both a personal and a family affair. This love of food is reflected in the wide selection of paper replica foods for the afterlife. Worshippers can acquire everything from sumptuous delicacies to simple comfort foods. Unsurprisingly, Cantonese cuisine features prominently: dim sum dishes, roast meats, seafoods, and desserts are as popular in death as in life. Unique Hong Kong foods, such as egg waffles, egg

亦大同小異。地府有發展完善的官僚架構，以玉皇為首，負責監督每項運作。因此，云云祭品中亦見各款身分文件。紙紮的冥府通行證使逝者能進入冥界，而冥府與陽間的護照式樣頗為相似，同樣印有個人資料和簽證頁。冥界的回鄉證（香港居民前往中國內地時使用的證件）允許鬼魂越過邊境，返回老家。紙製八達通方便死者在冥界乘坐的公共交通工具，還有旅遊巴士、火車和飛機的門票使先人更暢行無阻（有些祭祀者甚至會準備私人飛機或一隊客機），還會配合旅行保險單，使旅途更加安心。此外，駕駛執照、醫療卡和健身房會員證，亦可確保先人可在冥界使用最佳設施。

死者到達冥界後，必須找個棲身之所。在香港，自置物業可謂遙不可及的夢想，故此紙紮亦反映了居有定所的渴望。香港的樓價居全球之首，不少人畢生都為置業掙扎。除出極少數住在豪華公寓的幸運兒，城內仍然有成千上萬的基層人士住在如棺材般大小的「劏房」。這些分間單位多大如狹窄的單人床，不僅環境擠迫，還有結構和火警的危險。冥界的業權契約可保障先人在陰間也有個安樂窩，甚至令人羨慕的財產投資組合。豪華的別墅或大宅紙紮品，多以新界的複式村屋為藍本，而附有游泳池、花園和房屋保安的款式最為受歡迎。高樓大廈的單位儘管更為普遍，但幾乎從來沒有被製成紙祭品。不過，粗製的劏房紙紮亦見於至少一家紙號（資金短絀下的便宜替代品），香港苛刻的房屋市場也如實地在地府重現。

逝者離去時萬般帶不走,唯有身上穿著的衣服,各種風格和適合不同場合的紙紮衣服因此應運而生。從傳統中國服飾到現代街頭時裝,各式各樣的鞋子和配飾在紙紮店內應有盡有。紙紮店既有中國傳統風格的珠寶(仿玉或金),又有設計時尚的飾物。廣受歡迎的還有老花眼鏡、太陽眼鏡、手袋、手錶和鞋子。衣服和配飾可算是最貼心的禮物,不但能保死者舒適和安全,還讓他們在陰間展現獨特的穿衣風格。

滿足親人的基本生活所需後,祭祀者便轉向照料先人在冥界的通勤需求。穿梭香港水泄不通的街頭的豪華房車,也是大受歡迎的紙紮祭品。高性能汽車固然備受熱捧,但配有司機的經典英國轎車仍是信眾的首選。按實際比例製作的紙紮房車即使價格高昂,但仍廣受青睞。這些汽車通常用金箔或銀箔裝飾,再附上一個吉祥車牌號碼(模仿香港車牌的標準格式,即英國格式),有些甚至配有享負盛譽的製造商徽章,有些則用箔紙製成立體的引擎蓋為裝飾。批量生產和進口紙紮車約為一個鞋盒般的大小,價錢比較實惠。現時香港至少有一間紙號接受客人訂製大型紙紮貨車,即那些在城內運送海鮮、農產品等鮮活貨物的車輛。

紅磡福興隆紙料
Fook Hing Lung Papercrafts in Hung Hom

rolls and congee are found along with international fast foods and snacks. There are as many choices when it comes to drinks, from cognac to coffee. Horlicks and Ovaltine are both popular café drinks in Hong Kong, and paper replica tins can be found in most shops. Replica packages of teas are available, as well as teawares to brew them. And there are cooktops and refrigerators to furnish an after-life kitchen.

Replicas of the latest consumer electronics are also hot sellers. Hong Kong is among the most connected and hi-tech cities in the world. But technology for the afterlife is usually several models ahead of the latest worldly equivalents. On the other hand, papercraft stores offer laser-discs, VCR camcorders, and portable cassette players for older generations unfamiliar with newer devices. Accessories—cables, spare batteries, memory cards and the like—are also fashioned from paper. Replicas of transmission lines or mobile phone towers are never offered, which suggests that broader infrastructure is handled by the afterworld authorities.

Offerings for children embody the love of heartbroken families. They represent hope for a child's future in the next world and an opportunity to care for and dote on them. Over the years, families' offerings may change as their child grows up in the afterlife. For infants there are toys, bottles and formula. Older children might receive sports equipment or musical instruments. School supplies such as calculators, pencil cases, and composition books reflect the importance of education to Chinese parents. Even in the next life, children must study hard.

Offerings to grandparents and their generation are charming reminders of old Hong Kong: vacuum flasks decorated with rosy-cheeked cherubs or pink blossoms, simple 'kung fu' style slippers, abacuses, mahjong sets, wooden bird cages, vintage radios and old-style electric rice cookers. Paper 'fabrics' with floral

豪華遊艇成為常見的紙祭品。如同汽車那樣，有大型和小型可以選購。由本地紙紮工場量身訂造的漁船、舢舨、駁船和貨櫃船不斷來回往返於冥界碼頭。香港作為著名的海港，與海運相關的行業很自然也反映到在這個城市的紙紮品上。

飲食文化，是香港必不可少的重要一環，在生活上既是個人事宜，也是家庭事務。琳琅滿目的紙紮食品亦反映港人對美食的熱愛。從美味佳餚到簡單輕食，各式紙紮食品任君選擇，而粵菜則佔有很大比例，包括點心、燒肉、海鮮和甜點。這些美食在冥界的受歡迎程度並不比陽間遜色。雞蛋仔、蛋捲和粥等香港特色美食，以及西方快餐和小吃都可以在紙號找到。由干邑到咖啡，飲料的種類亦多不勝數，當中不乏好立克和阿華田等茶餐廳飲料。紙號亦有提供茶包，以及沖茶用的茶具，還有供先人在冥界布置廚房的爐灶和雪櫃。

最新型號的電子產品也是非常暢銷的紙紮祭品。香港是全球通訊最緊密的高科技城市之一，但冥界的科技常領先於陽間的同類產品。紙號亦為不熟悉新科技的老一輩提供了激光影碟、便攜式攝像機和盒帶播放器，其附件如電線、備用電池、記憶卡等也是由紙製成。然而，紙紮製品中卻從未見傳輸線或手機訊號發射站，意味廣泛的基礎設施還是由地府當局管理。

祭祀小孩的紙紮品，讓傷心欲絕的家人投射對孩子來世的期許，也是他們照顧和寵愛孩子的最後機會，深深體

荃灣天成行香燭紙業

Tin Shing Hong Worshipping Supplies in Tsuen Wan

現了切膚之痛中的愛。隨著孩子在冥界成長，親人每年也可準備不同的祭品。親人會為嬰兒選購玩具、奶瓶和奶粉。年長一點的孩子可能會收到運動器材或樂器。計算機、筆盒和習作本等學校用品亦反映華人家庭對教育的重視。即使在陰間，孩子也必須用功學習。

切合祖父母之輩的紙紮品總令人想起昔日的香港。玫瑰腮紅色或粉紅色花朵裝飾的保溫杯、俗稱「功夫鞋」的免綁帶黑布鞋、算盤、麻雀牌、木製鳥籠、老式收音機和舊式電飯煲。帶有花卉圖案和柔和色彩的紙「布匹」，則供母親或祖母縫製衣服。這些懷舊的設計充滿六、七十年代香港製造業的標誌性美學，令人懷緬過去繁榮昌盛的時代。

隨著時間推移，紙祭品的種類儘管沒太大改變，但紙號仍然不斷推陳出新，代步的馬匹換成汽車，金條也加入鈔票和信用卡成為資產之選。近年，傳真和傳呼機也被智能手機和筆記本電腦取而代之。除了旗袍等中國傳統服裝外，也添加了各種現代風格的服飾，包括金色西裝和情趣內衣。

motifs and pastel colours are offered to mothers or grandmothers for them to make their own clothes. These nostalgic designs embody the iconic aesthetic of Hong Kong's manufacturing boom of the sixties and seventies and recall a bygone era.

Though the types of offerings remain more or less constant over time, papercraft sellers are always updating their selection. With the passing of time, horses have made way for cars, and gold bars have been joined by banknotes and credit cards. More recently, faxes and pagers have been replaced by smartphones and laptops. And traditional Chinese clothing, such as cheongsams, have been complemented by all manner of modern styles, including gold suits and racy lingerie. While some offerings remain perennial favourites, others reflect trends or passing fads. Foods like sushi, macarons, and swiss chocolates have appeared in recent years. In fact, paper replicas of food are themselves a relatively recent development. Real foods—usually fruits, buns and roast birds—remain important offerings. But they are often supplemented with a much wider variety of paper replica foods. Pets have become a feature of the modern selection of offerings. Owning the latest trendy breed is a sign of status and wealth (so a natural choice for an offering), and pets also guarantee companionship and love in the afterlife. Offerings for pets themselves have even become popular. The constant changes not only promise that a visit to the paper shop will always be interesting, it also means that paper offerings are always evolving to reflect the city's trends and tastes.

Life in Hong Kong is characterised by two contradictory preoccupations: saving and consuming. But, when it comes to paper offerings, the dead are not forced to choose. The low price of spirit money and of paper replicas makes it possible to offer both in huge amounts. Hong Kong's wealth is concentrated in the hands of a few (one in seven residents is a millionaire, while one in five lives in

有些紙紮常年備受青睞，而其他製品則反映時下的潮流或過時的時尚。壽司、馬卡龍和瑞士巧克力等紙紮食品近年相繼面世。事實上，紙紮食品亦是相對較新的產品。如水果、麵包和燒臘等真正的食物，仍是不可或缺的祭品輔以各式各樣的紙紮食品祭祀。寵物已成為現今特色紙紮，當中最潮流的品種視為地位和財富的象徵，自然大受歡迎。寵物亦能在冥界陪伴和關愛，而贈予寵物的紙紮祭品也相當受歡迎。日新月異的紙紮產品不僅增添行逛紙號時的趣味，也反映了香港不停演變的潮流和品味。

在香港的生活，不免陷入儲蓄和消費的兩難，但就紙紮而言，先人不用面對二選一的決擇。冥錢和祭品的低廉價格，即使大肆選購，也不用傾家蕩產。香港的財富集中在極少數人手中（每七人中就有一名百萬富翁，每五人中便有一人活於貧窮線下）。不管生前的經濟狀況如何，先人在冥界所擁有的奢侈品都遠較在世時擁有的奢華得多。祭祀者均希望，死者輪迴轉世時能晉身上流圈子。為此，先人會定期收到無窮無盡的紙錢和代表身分象徵的物品。喪葬的紙紮祭品中，常包括數不止一個重塑整條購物大道的大型立體模型，使死者能在來生成為腰纏萬貫和受人尊敬的業主。如此慷慨的施予，為先人和生者都招來好運和面子。

在傳統中國社會，僱用家僕象徵財富和社會地位，而紙紮僕人一直是葬禮上典型的祭品。外籍家庭傭工，又稱

poverty). But regardless of their financial position in this world, the residents of the afterlife are lavished with luxuries far more extravagant than they could have enjoyed in their former lives. Worshippers believe it is important that the dead are accepted into affluent circles in the next life. To this end, they receive endless piles of cash and a steady supply of status symbols. Funeral offerings may include large-scale dioramas of entire streets, with properties and shops, for the deceased to become a prosperous and respected business owner or landlord in the next life. Such largesse earns good fortune and prestige for the recipient and the giver alike.

Servants were traditionally a sign of wealth and social standing in Chinese society, and paper servants remain a standard offering at funerals. Domestic workers, or 'helpers', are a longstanding feature of Hong Kong society. Until recently, they were usually older Chinese women. These days they are almost all young women from the Philippines and Indonesia. One in ten Hong Kong workers, around five percent of the city's population, is a foreign domestic worker. Compared with other foreign workers they have stricter visa conditions, a lower minimum wage, and worse working conditions. They also suffer high rates of abuse. With this in mind, there is something unsettling about seeing paper servants piled in with paper refrigerators and paper televisions.

Well-known fashion labels and luxury brands adorn countless paper replicas. A paper handbag with a Louis Vuitton or Chanel label, though still not expensive, costs more than an otherwise identical offering. In recent years, global fashion labels have served warnings to Hong Kong's paper sellers. These powerful luxury brands have long sought to stamp out Hong Kong's knockoff clothes, shoes and bags for the living. But they have only recently turned their attention to offerings for the dead. Some sellers defiantly suggested the warning letters should be re-addressed and burned for the lawyers

「工人姐姐」，是支持香港社會已久的重要一員。家傭以往常由年長的中國女性擔當，如今幾乎全都是來自菲律賓和印尼的年輕女性。在香港每十名勞工就有一名是外籍家庭傭工，佔全港人口約百分之五。與其他外傭相比，他們要面對更嚴格的簽證條件、更低的最低工資、更惡劣的工作條件，當中不少人還屢遭虐待。想到這一點，看著眼前一個個紙紮傭人置身於紙雪櫃和紙電視中，不禁心感不自在。

知名時裝和奢侈品牌是無數紙紮的模仿對象。印有路易威登或香奈兒標誌的紙紮手袋雖遠不及本物昂貴，但其價格卻高於其他一式一樣的紙紮手袋。近年，不少國際時裝品牌都曾向香港的紙紮銷售商發出警告。這些奢侈品牌向來致力打擊在港的冒牌服裝、鞋子和手袋，直至最近才轉向狙擊獻給死者的紙紮祭品。有些賣家曾大膽要求品牌重寫警告信的地址，並燒給冥府的律師處理。在受到本地社群和國際媒體的嚴厲批評後，這些跨國公司迅速撤銷控告。然而，經營困難的紙號始終難以負擔訴訟，更多商店自此對仿製品牌的設計避之則吉。

相比奢侈堂皇的製作，實而不華的祭品也能反映中國文化裏的陰間，有別於與其他文化中的完美天堂。座枱式電風扇、冷氣機、暖爐和雨傘用以應對氣候的需要，拐杖、老花鏡、化妝品、膠布、假牙、助聽器、止痕藥膏和按摩椅仍大有需要。印有香港老牌商標的傳統中藥，保證有效紓緩痛楚。更換電池、給電子產品充電、熨衣服、清潔牙

of the spirit world to deal with. After being sharply criticised by the local community and international media, these multinational companies quickly withdrew. Nevertheless, struggling papercraft stores can ill afford a lawsuit, and many now shy away from imitating brand names.

In contrast to extravagant and showy offerings, many offerings are pragmatic and humdrum, suggesting that the Chinese after-life is quite unlike the perfect heavens of some other cultures. Its climate requires desk-fans, heaters, air-conditioners and umbrellas. Its residents remain in need of walking sticks, reading glasses, cosmetics, bandages, false teeth, hearing aids, insect-bite cream and massage chairs. Traditional herbal remedies, with familiar labels of old Hong Kong brands, promise to soothe aches and pains. Even in death there is no escape from tedium—batteries must be replaced, devices must be charged, clothing must be ironed, teeth must be cleaned. Though these mundane offerings paint a dull picture of the afterlife, they reveal a touching attentiveness to the comfort of the deceased.

Papercraft makers are similarly attentive to small details when crafting offerings—fast food meals come with salt and pepper sachets, glasses come with protective cases, and razors come with replacement blades. The care taken by papercraft makers to attend to these small details not only makes the replicas more relatable, but fills in the outline of heaven itself, creating a tangible vision of the afterlife that gives comfort to the bereaved. Death is like moving into an unfurnished house, with the funeral as housewarming. Gifts continue to be sent on anniversaries, and the living and the dead keep in touch through dreams and prayers. Heaven is only slightly more distant than San Francisco or Singapore.

齒——人死後也無法逃避繁瑣的生活細節。儘管這些平平無奇的祭品呈現了一個沉悶的陰間，卻顯示後人期望死者能舒適安居的細心關懷。

不同師傅在製作紙紮時同樣注重細節，如快餐食品附有小袋餐鹽和黑椒、眼鏡配有眼鏡盒、剃鬚刀備有更換刀片。師傅用心對待每一個微小的細節，不僅使祭品更容易引起共鳴，也圓滿了在冥府生活的種種想像，為逝者的親友帶來一絲安慰。死亡就如喬遷，而葬禮就像是新居入伙的慶宴。生者每逢週年紀念日會為逝者送上禮物，平日則通過夢境來保持聯繫。先人與後人之距離，僅比美加稍遠一點。

進口的大路紙紮祭品近年愈見普遍。這些批量生產的進口商品雖然製作成本較低，但甚少能捕捉本地產品的神髓。較顯而易見的遺漏包括繁體字（中國大陸用簡體字）和英國標準的插頭。其他細節上的疏忽（這個城市中獨一無二的細節和特質）並非那麼明顯，但卻使人更強烈感受到本土特質的缺席。

此攝影集用了六年時間收集紙紮祭品。這些製作者不詳的現成祭品，來自香港多區：上環、油麻地、紅磡、旺角、深水埗、長沙灣和荃灣。在短短數年間，手工製作的紙紮變得越發罕見，許多店鋪和工場均相繼結業。與其他傳統手工藝品一樣，紙紮行業已成為租金上漲、大量進口批量產品和習俗變遷的受害者。為防止火災和改善空氣質

These days, generic imported paper replicas are increasingly common. Though cheaper to make, these mass-produced imports lack the distinctive qualities of the real-world objects found in Hong Kong. Some of these are obvious features, such as the traditional form of Chinese characters (now abandoned on the mainland), or the British standard electrical plug. Others—small details and minor idiosyncrasies unique to the city—are less obvious, but their absence can be felt even more keenly.

The paper offerings photographed in this book were collected over the past six years. They are premade offerings, and their makers are unidentified. They come from neighbourhoods across Hong Kong: Sheung Wan, Yau Ma Tei, Hung Hom, Mong Kok, Sham Shui Po, Cheung Sha Wan and Tsuen Wan. In this short time, handmade offerings have become harder to find, and many shops and workrooms have closed down. Along with many of Hong Kong's traditional crafts, the industry has fallen victim to rising rents, mass-produced imports and changing customs. Laws to prevent fires and improve air quality, as well as stricter housing management rules, prohibit burning paper offerings in many homes and streets. Worshippers can now buy offerings cheaply online from outside of Hong Kong—with the option to even outsource the burning. Most of the city's papercraft makers have closed up shop or moved their workrooms to neighbouring mainland provinces, and only a handful of local masters continue to fill custom orders. As younger Hong Kongers leave behind the traditions of their grandparents, apprentices are not filling the retiring masters' shoes. Many in the trade feel that, like the paper offerings they craft, their industry is not long for this world.

Though it may be fading from daily life, the custom of burning paper offerings lives on. The ritual offers a moment to contemplate in a city of relentless enterprise; a time to think fondly of departed

紅磡裕興隆紙號

Yue Hing Loong
Offerings in
Hung Hom

loved ones; and a time to live the customs and values that continue to define Hong Kong. It brings families together, and affirms the importance of honouring parents and elders in this life and the next —teachings ingrained in Chinese life since the time of Confucius.

And so, piece by piece, an entire city of paper continues to float across worlds, with each offering becoming part of an ever richer and more colourful vision of Hong Kong in the next life.

素而立的法例，以及更嚴格的住屋規管，禁止信眾在街上多處和家中焚燒祭品。另外，祭祀者現在可以在網上以低廉的價格，從海外訂購祭品，甚至可選擇外判燒衣的服務。不少香港的紙號經已倒閉，或將其工場移至鄰近的中國大陸省分。只餘碩果僅存的本地師傅，堅持製作客人訂製的紙紮品。隨著香港祖輩的傳統被年輕一代遺忘，這個行業亦難免青黃不接。業內人士均認為，一如終需化灰的祭品，紙紮這行業大抵也不久於世。

燒衣或會漸漸消失於街頭，但燃燒紙紮的習俗仍得以薪火相傳。在分秒必爭的香港，這個儀式提供了沉靜思考的片刻，追憶逝去的親人，還可藉此感受本土風俗和價值。祭祀習俗把家人聚在一起，重溫了時刻尊敬父母和長輩的重要性，正正是根深蒂固於中國文化中的儒家教誨。

紙紮一件燒、一件現，化作煙縷穿越人間與冥界，在另一個國度建構一個更豐富多彩的香港。

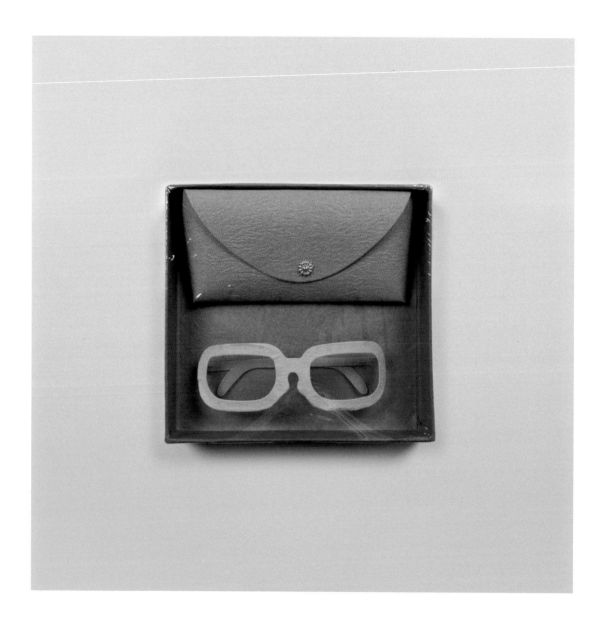

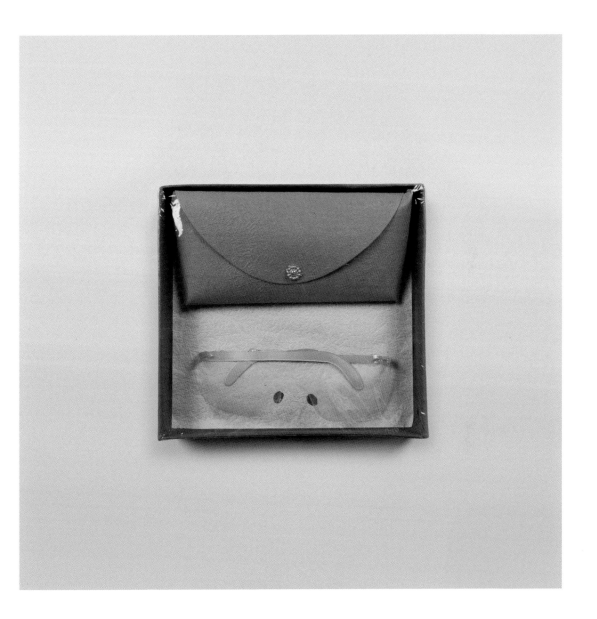

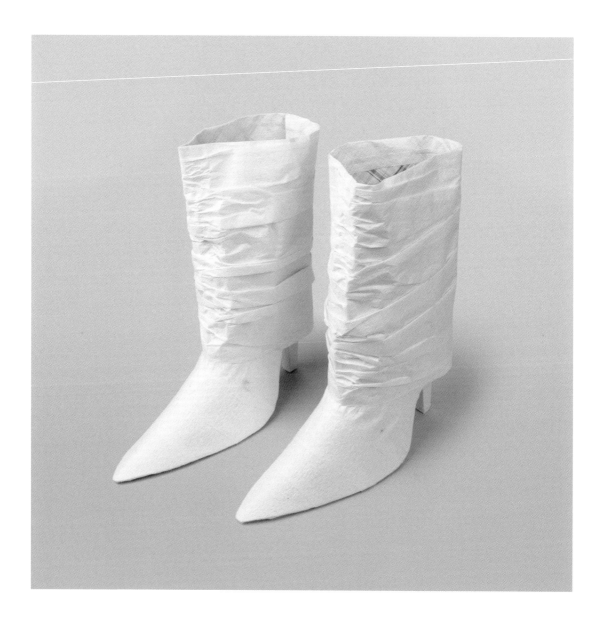

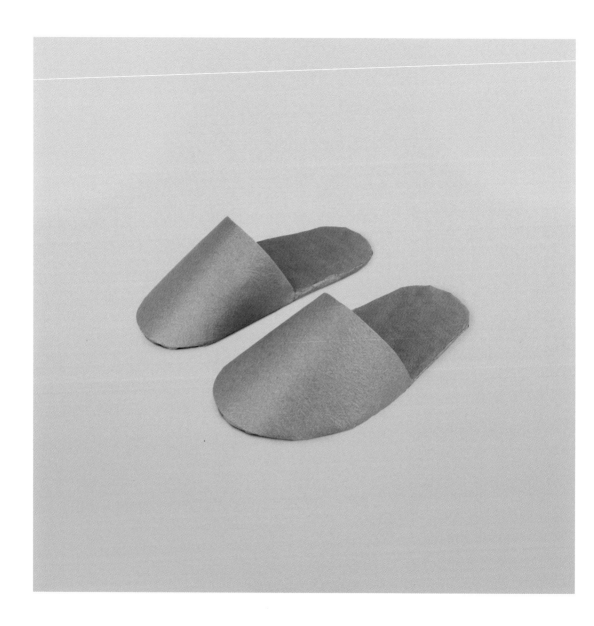

49

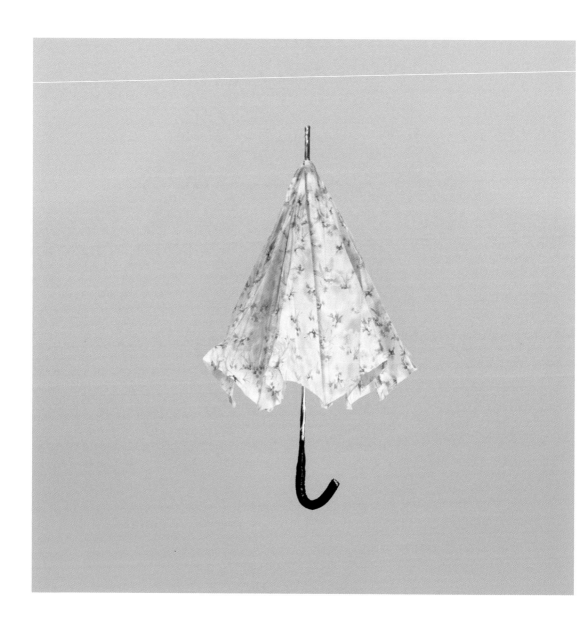

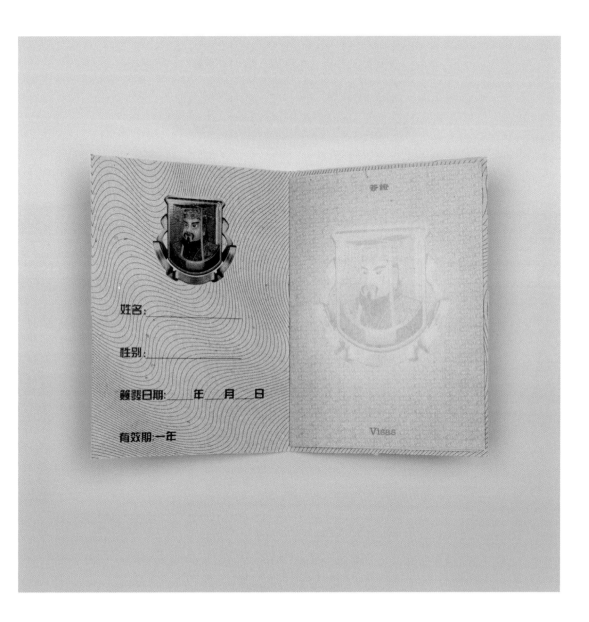

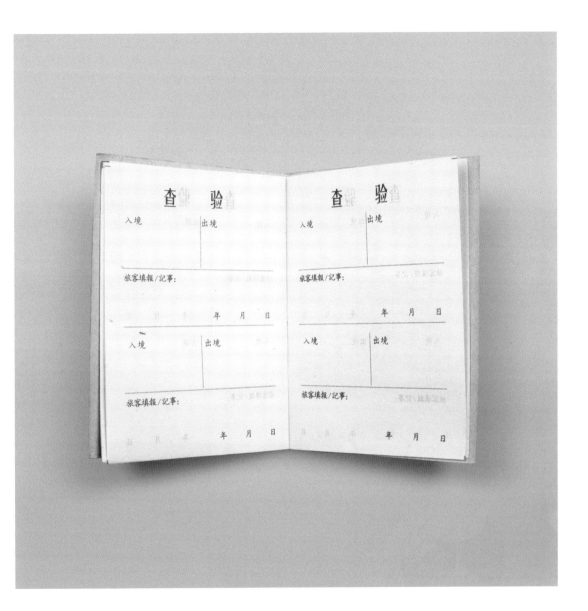

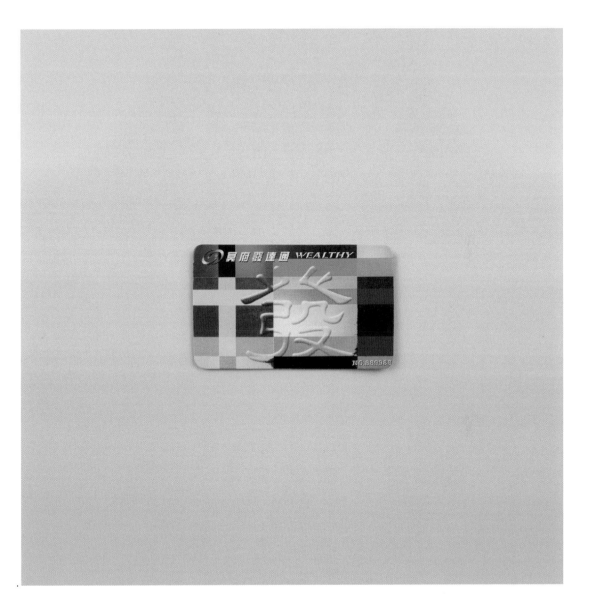

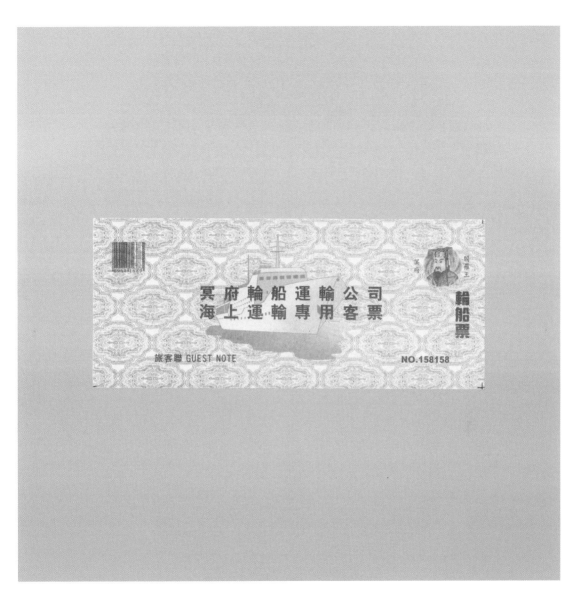

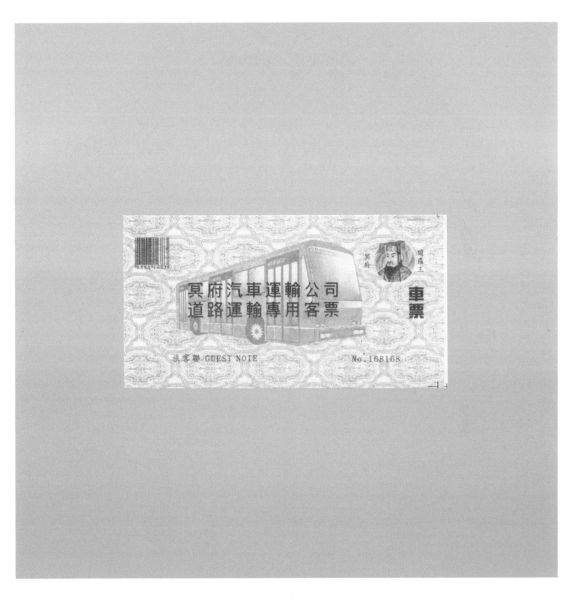

66

冥通銀行
支票存根

附加信息: ....
....
....
....

出票日期: 　　年　月　日
收款人: ....
金額: ....
....
8888 888888 88888

付款期限自出票之日起十天

冥通　銀行
THE BANK OF HELL

出票日期: 　　年　月　日　　　　　　　出票人帳號: ....

收款人: ....

冥 幣: ....

8888 888888 88888

上列款項請從
我賬戶內支付
出票人簽章: ....

71

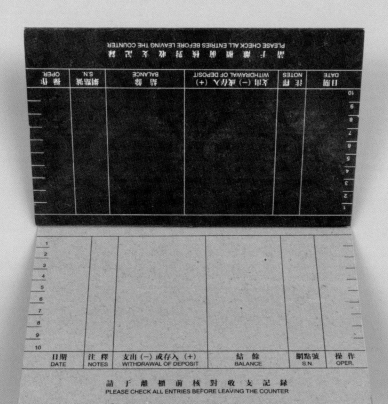

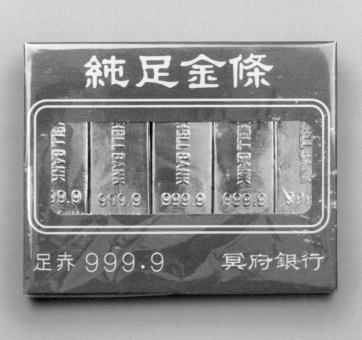

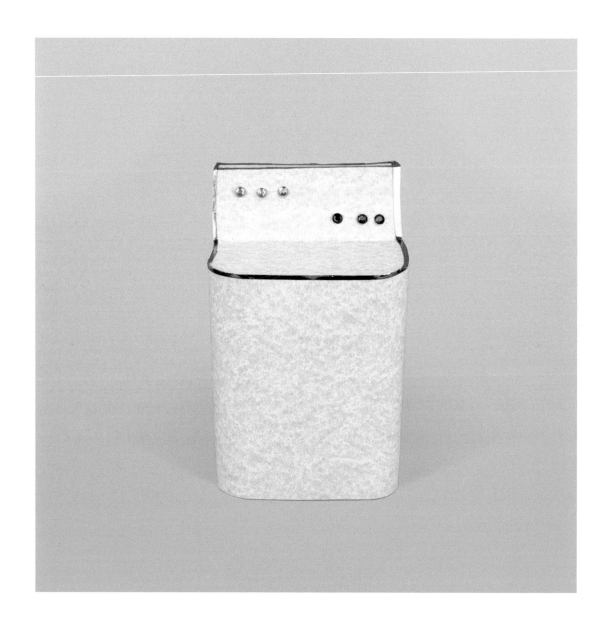

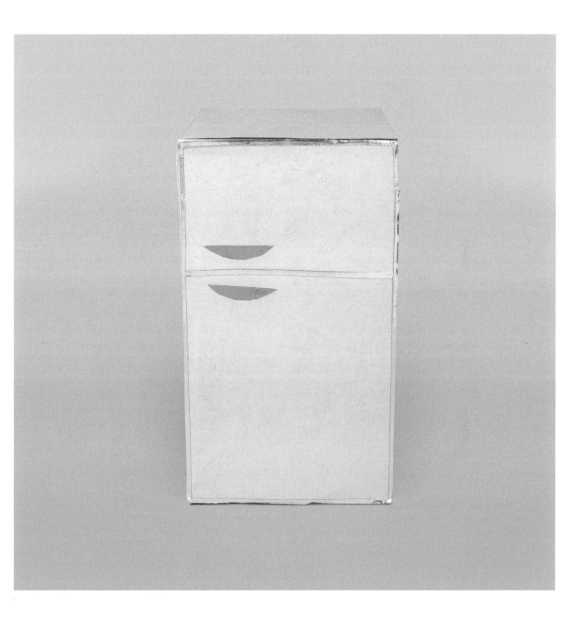

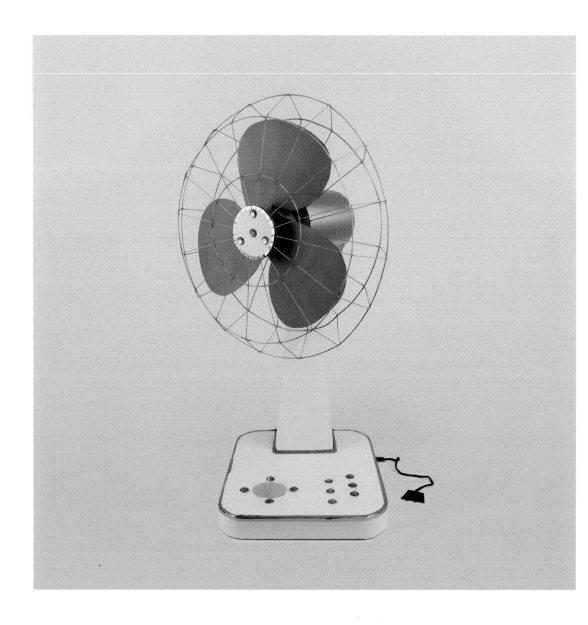

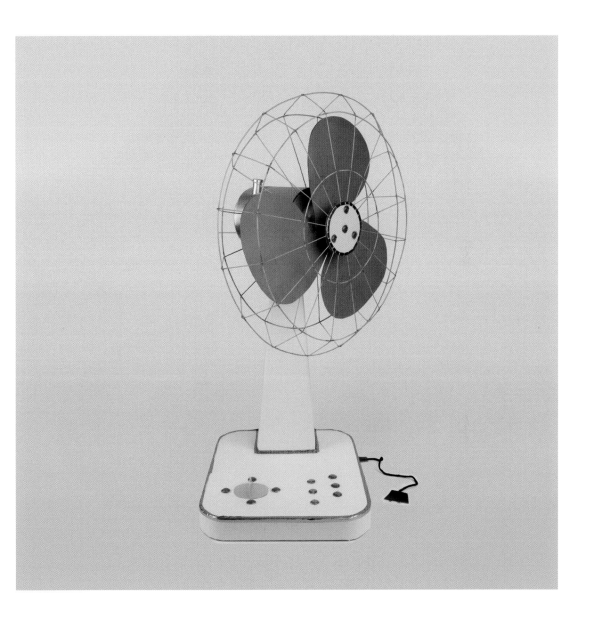

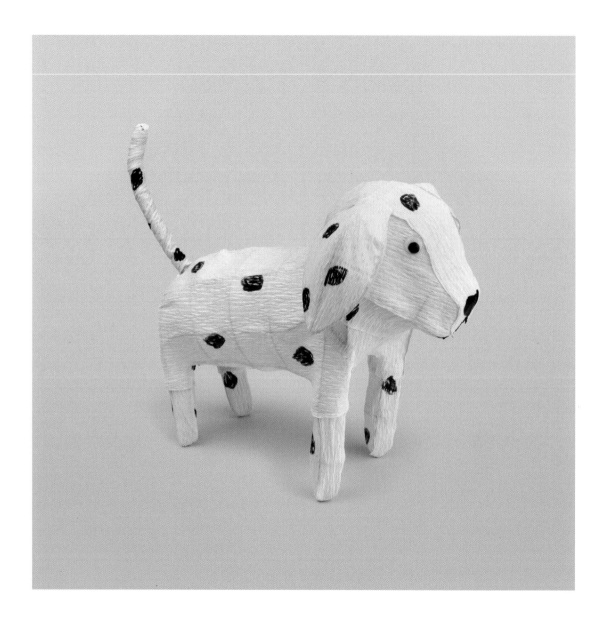

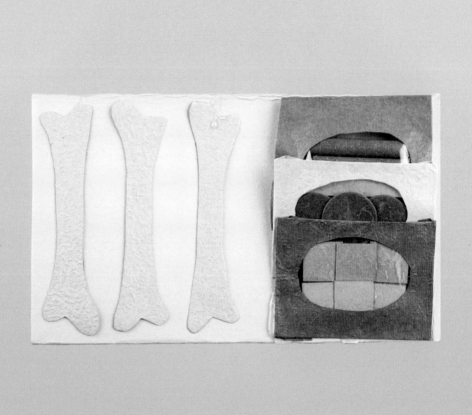

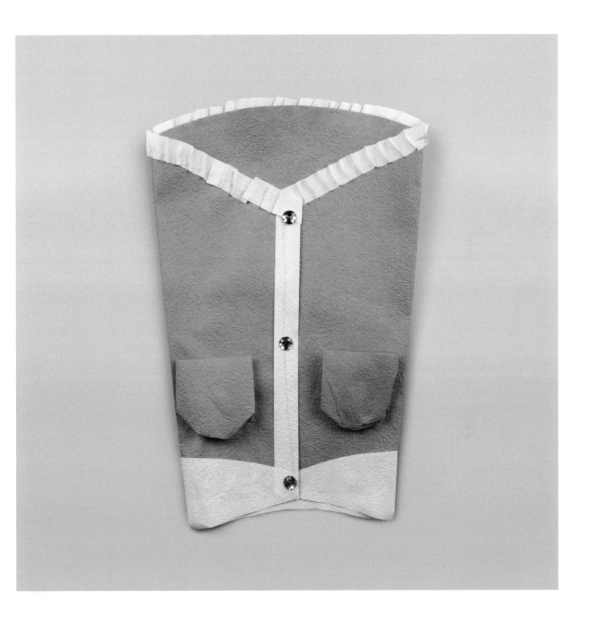

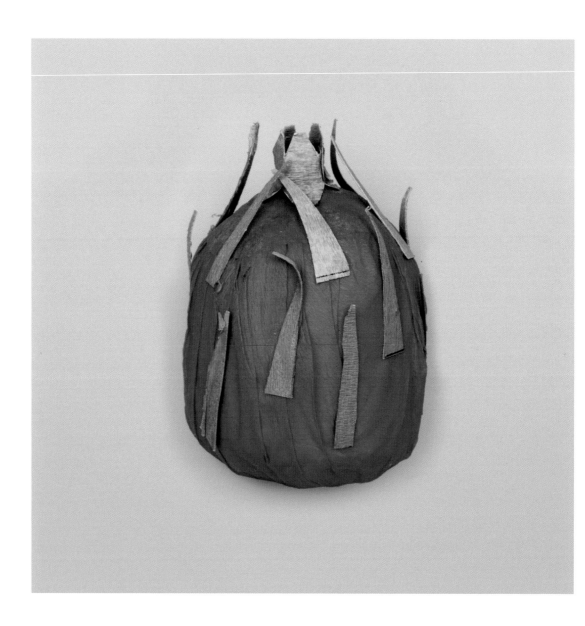

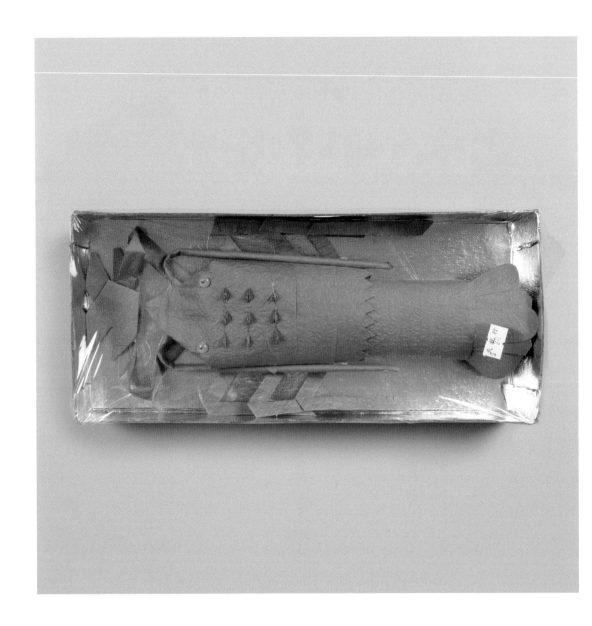

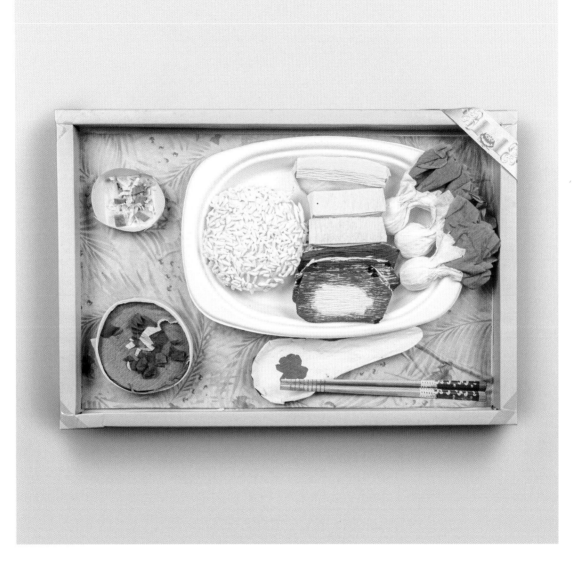

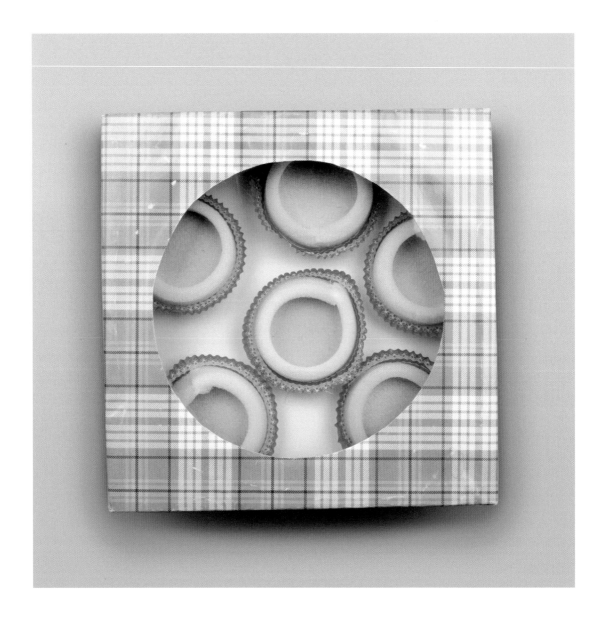

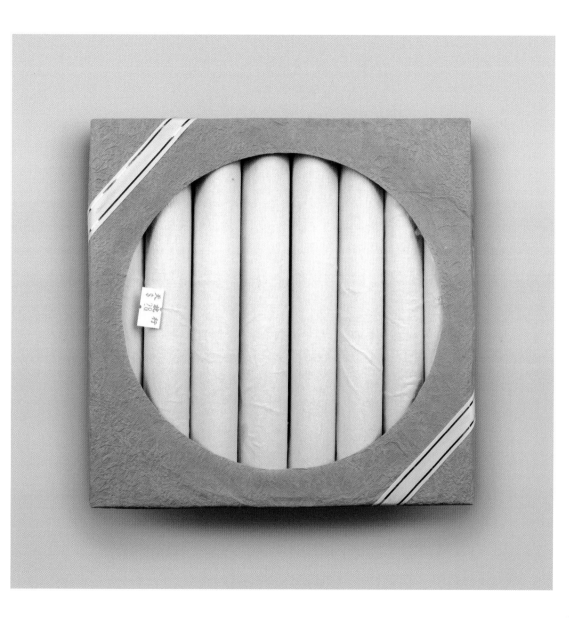

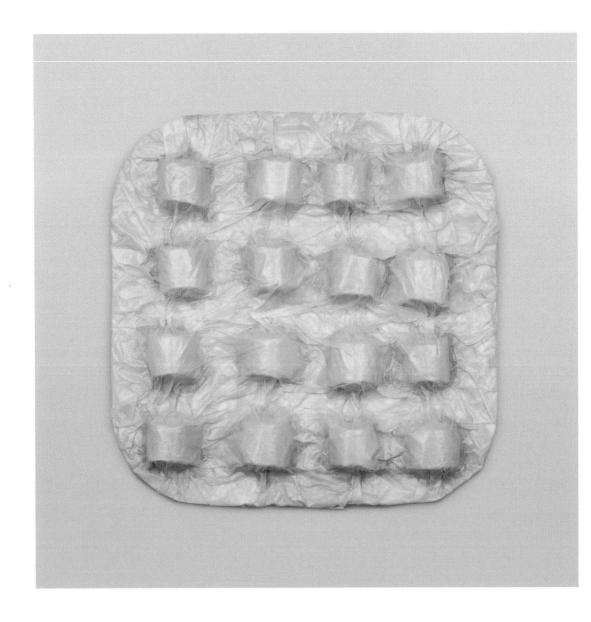

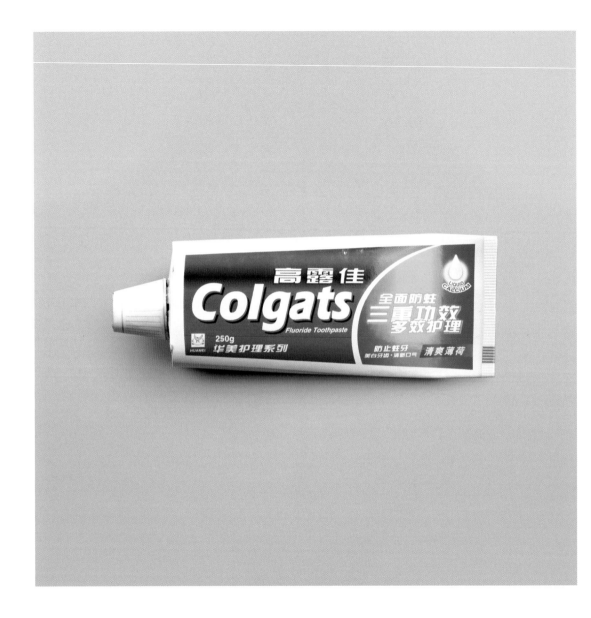

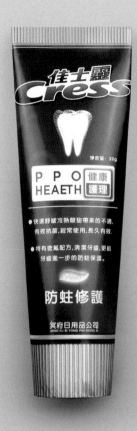

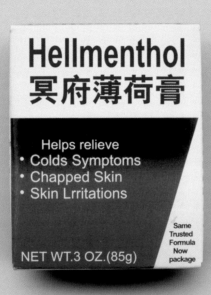

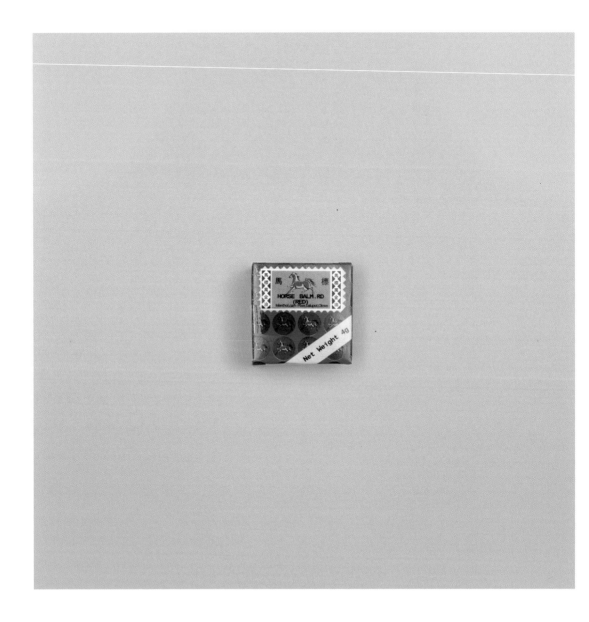

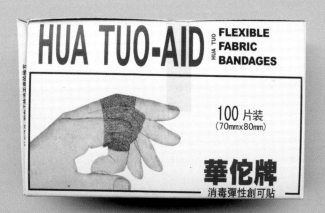

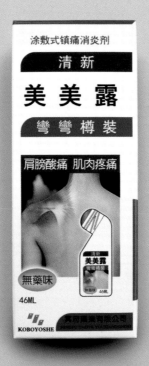

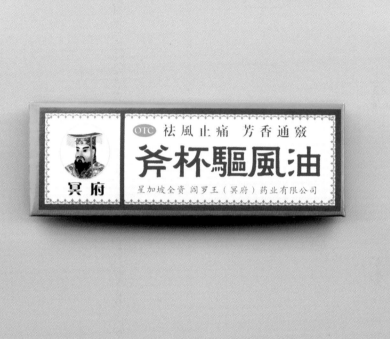

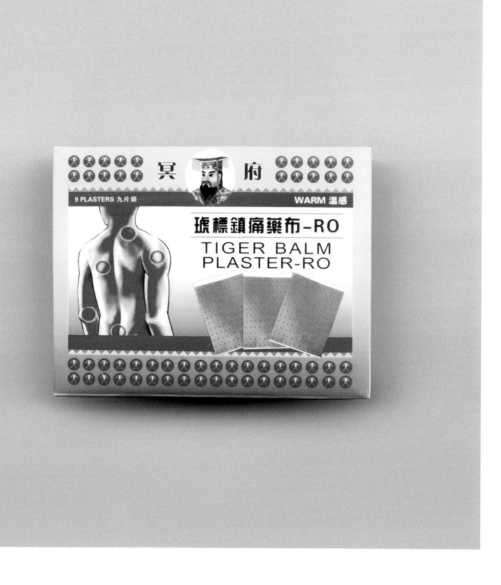

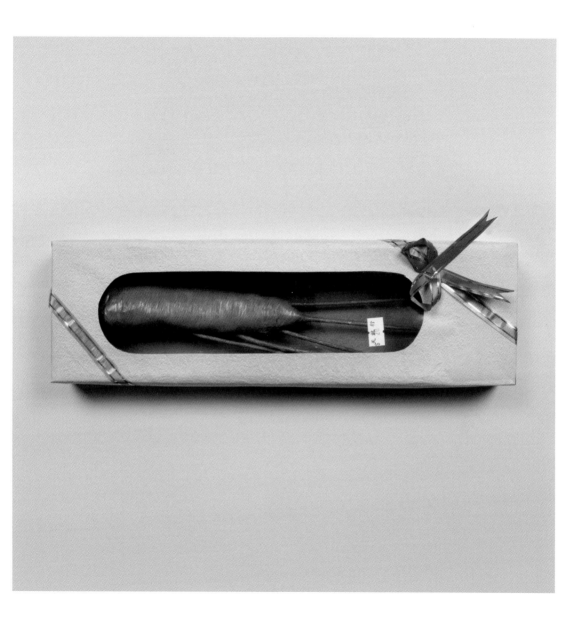

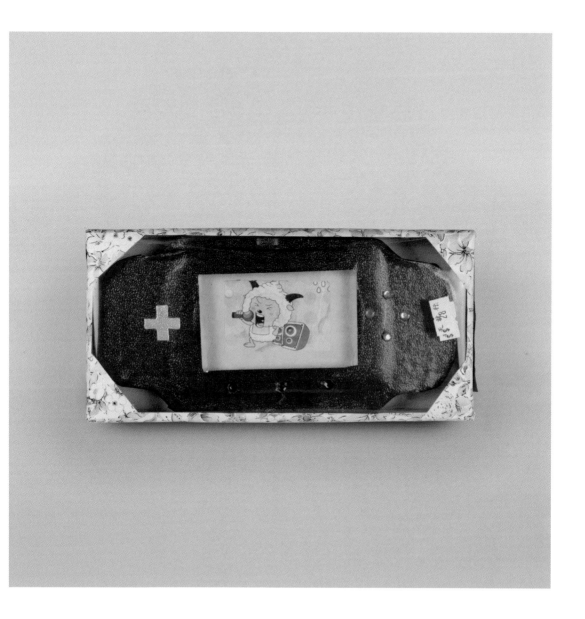

169

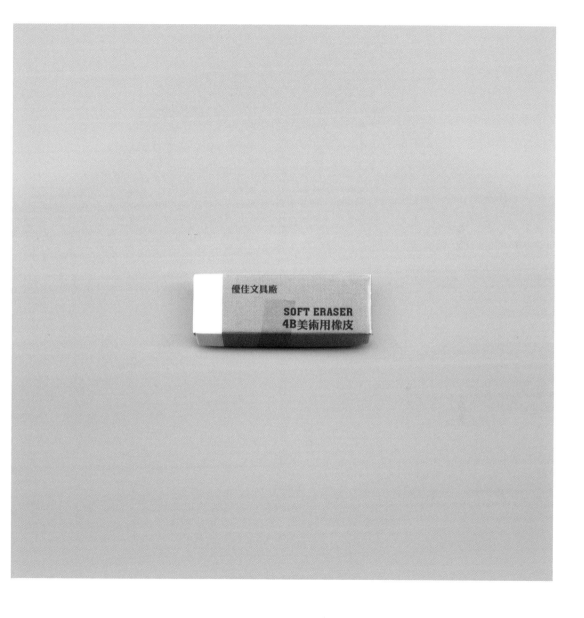

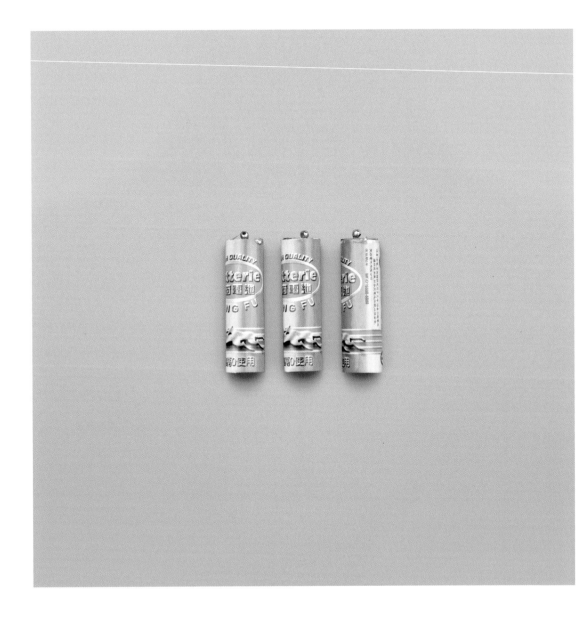

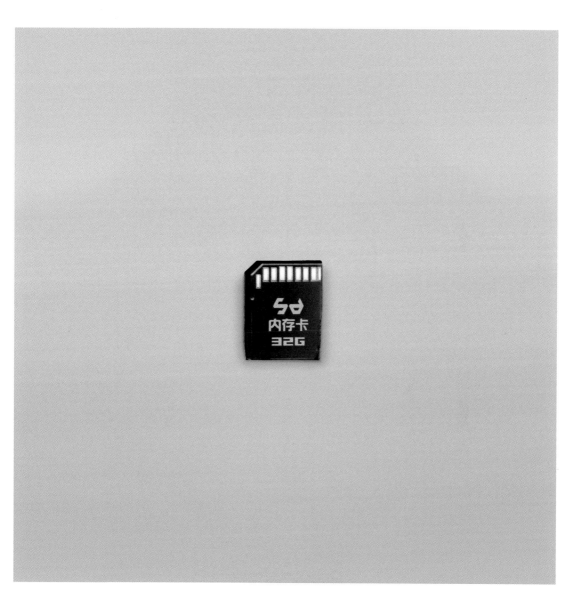

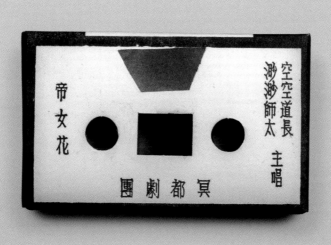

Paper Offerings Have Much More to Offer

Rosanna Li Wei-han

I have lived in Hung Hom since I was a child. There are three funeral homes in this old neighbourhood, and a thriving funeral district in the streets around them. There are the 'longevity shops' that sell coffins, florists selling wreaths, and sales rooms for funeral homes. There are shops for headstones, burial urns, burial shrouds, incense and candles, mourning garments, and shops for paper offerings. There are also many Taoist temples and altars where mourners can pray and perform rites. Unsurprisingly then, most Hung Hom locals are not concerned with taboos about death. But other Hong Kongers, suffice to say, are somewhat more troubled! When coming by taxi to the Universal Funeral Home to make arrangements or to attend a memorial, hardly anyone dares mention it by name. Rather, they ask for 'The Grand Hotel'—its euphemistic pseudonym. As for me, when I take a taxi home or book a Lalamove or a GoGoVan, I do the same—the directions are just as clear, and the driver won't feel so apprehensive about the destination!

When I was little, I loved wandering the streets near my home. I was most attracted to the paper offerings shops, not for any reason other than that they were often 'three in one' shops that also sold stationery and toys. For a young child, not even a lolly shop or a video

點只衣紙咁簡單 [1]

李慧嫻

　　我自小住在紅磡老區，區內有三間殯儀館；而附近有幾條街，亦是殯儀行業集中之地——如長生店（棺木鋪）、碑石店、骨灰盅店、壽衣店、鮮花店、香燭店、孝服店和紙紮鋪等，成行成市。此外，道觀及神庵亦不少。區內居民，大都（無奈被）百無禁忌，但區外人呢？多少有些忌諱吧！聽說一般乘的士前來辦喪事或送殯的人，很少會直接告訴司機：「唔該，『世界殯儀館』。」而是說：「唔該，『大酒店』。」「大酒店」就是殯儀館的代名詞。而我呢，為保證司機安心行駛，我乘坐的士回家或召喚 Lalamove 或 GoGoVan 等小型客貨車時，也只會跟司機大哥說：「地點就在『大酒店』附近呀！」這樣說，路就好找了，司機也不會猶豫了！

　　小時最愛在家居附近的街道蹓躂，最吸引我的是紙鋪，不為什麼，只因為這些店鋪不單純出售紙紮，而往往是兼售文具和玩具的三合一商店。對小孩和學生來說，

arcade could be more enthralling—I would often lose myself and forget to go home. Over time, the three seemed to blend together. In my eyes stationery was toys and toys were paper offerings. And among the selection of paper offerings there were even replicas of stationery and replicas of toys—a true three-in-one.

There were all kinds of paper offerings related to the basic necessities and pleasures of everyday life. Small pieces were made of pasted paper, while large offerings were made of a bamboo frame and then covered in coloured paper. Generally, they were made from glossy wax paper or from more flexible crepe paper. The eye-catching colours were those commonly used during traditional festivals: bright reds, yellows, purples, greens, as well as gold and silver. This paper was made into beautiful paper cups, bowls and dishes, paper clothes, shoes and socks, coffee tables and chairs, sweets, dried fruits, wine and cigarettes. These items were about the same size as their real-life counterparts, yet they were not 'real'. So who were they made for? My family wasn't Buddhist or Taoist. We didn't keep ancestral tablets or worship the gods of Chinese folk religion. My primary and secondary schooling was Catholic. All I knew of 'burning clothes' (a common name for the paper offering ritual) was that paper clothes are burned and given to the deceased. As far as I was aware, paper offerings seemed more like toys.

My favourite class in primary school was handicrafts, where our teacher taught us to make paper toys, such as houses, cars, boats, clothes and puppets. As well as using cardboard, we also used the same glossy paper and crepe paper that I had seen in the paper offerings shop. After class, I would bring my completed handicrafts home and play with them. And so, my understanding was that paper offerings and paper toys were one and the same. When I was in secondary school, I took part in school drama performances, and was responsible for making the stage props. It struck me that the

除了糖果店和遊戲機鋪外，也想不到比這類三合一店鋪更吸引的了。我常耽在鋪內樂而忘返，久而久之在我眼內，文具是玩具，玩具是紙紮，紙紮中有文具亦有玩具，名符其實的三合一。紙紮品種繁多，均與日常生活、衣食住行、娛樂等有關。小件全是紙糊的，大的則先以竹篾紮個骨架，然後才糊上彩紙，一般使用反光蠟光紙或有少許彈性的縐紙，顏色鮮艷、全是傳統節慶時最常用的紅、黃、紫、綠、金和銀等色調，十分奪目。它們被製作成漂亮的杯盆碗碟、衣履鞋襪、茶几椅子、糖果餅乾、洋酒香煙等，大小比例和真的品種差不多，但又不是真的，那究竟是給誰使用的呢？我家不唸佛、不信道，也沒有祖先靈位、也不拜地主、灶君等。由小學到中學，就讀天主教學校，故對「燒衣」概念甚為模糊，不甚了了，只知道衣紙是燒掉送給逝者的。自覺紙品更像玩具。小學時最喜歡勞作科。上課時，老師教我們用紙張製作玩具，有房屋、車船、衣著和木偶等。材料除了硬咭紙外，便是上述的七彩蠟光紙和縐紙了。下課後就把完成的勞作帶回家耍玩。所以在我的理解中，衣紙玩具同一物。中學時參加校內話劇表演，每多負責舞台道具製作，那時又覺道具如紙紮，設計和造法都差不多。

　　中學後，我考上教育學院的美術科。畢業後在一所中學任教美術和設計科。噢！教學大綱也包括紙藝創作，有時會要求學生收集些包裝電視機、洗衣機或雪櫃等的大型

props were like paper offerings, and that the design and fabrication methods were more or less the same.

After finishing secondary school, I was admitted to the Fine Arts Department of the Institute of Education, and, after graduating, I taught art and design in a secondary school. *Oh!* The syllabus also included papercraft! Sometimes I would ask students to collect cardboard boxes from televisions, washing machines, or refrigerators and cut them up to make giant robots, buildings, or buses. Or I would teach them to use paper card to design clothing, shoes, accessories or greeting cards. The difference between these activities and my primary school handicrafts class was that they were focused on understanding design elements like colour, form, proportion, and texture. Later, I taught at the School of Design at Hong Kong Polytechnic University; first design fundamentals and later product design. As my students experimented with their design ideas, they would use paper to make prototypes. *Ha-ha-ha!* Perhaps this is my personal secret: looking at these paper proto- types inevitably brought back memories of my childhood!

After growing up, I kept living in Hung Hom. My work as a teacher kept me busy. Though I would walk past the offering shops, I didn't stop to go inside. The stationery and toys no longer held such interest for me, but the colourful paper offerings—tied as they were to my teaching—would always catch my attention.

One day, I noticed that a tiny paper offerings shop had opened opposite my building. I passed it each day on my way to and from work. To accompany the little shop's opening, the owner held a big opening sale. A small box of paper sandals was put by the shopfront, with a note: *'Special price: this summer's latest sandal styles'.* It never occurred to me that a paper offering shop would use the same techniques to attract customers as a regular shop! Being such a bargain, I stopped to take a look and, sure enough,

瓦坑紙盒，加以切割、組合設計成機械巨人、樓房、巴士模型等。有時則教學生以紙咭設計服式、鞋類、飾物和賀咭等。跟我小學勞作科不同的地方是，他們主要透過製作紙品來學習設計元素：色彩、圖案、比例、質感等。後來我進了香港理工大學設計學院教書，先後教授設計基礎和產品設計課程，學生們在試驗設計意念過程中，運用紙張來做樣板……呵呵呵！也許這是我的個人秘密，看著這些樣板，有時難免帶起我的童年回憶！

成長後，仍居紅磡。教學工作忙，走在街上，紙紮鋪仍在，但也只是匆匆而過，店中文具和玩具再不大吸引，但基於和我教學上的千絲萬縷的關係，還是會對彩色衣紙再三回眸。

其後某年某月，忽然發現住所對面新開了間小小的紙紮鋪，乃每天上、下班必經之路。小店新張期間，舉行「益街坊大減價」，門前放了一小箱紙品涼鞋，鞋中插有一紙牌，上寫「特價今夏最新款涼鞋」。沒想到紙紮鋪也會運用一般商店營銷手法以吸引顧客！既是平賣，我駐足而觀，果然中伏，我把那箱紙品涼鞋全數購入。這些紙鞋運用電腦素描及 Photoshop 等修圖設計技術，以人手及機械合成，款式逼真時尚，越看越愛、越難放手。此後有一段時間，常在那小店購入新上市的紙鞋。

此外，空閒時我常在區內的紙紮鋪流連，看看有沒有衣紙新貨。不時在店內遇到為先人挑選紙品的顧客，

I bought the entire box. These paper shoes were created using a mix of handcraft and digital graphics methods like digital sketching and Photoshop. The result was quite convincing and fashionable. The more I looked at them the more I loved them and found them hard to put down. For a time after, I often bought the latest paper shoes from that little shop.

In my spare time, I've often hung around in the local paper shops to see if there are new offerings for sale. Now and then, I come across customers choosing paper offerings for their ancestors, and overhear their conversations with the shopkeeper:

'Do you have the new model of this phone?'

'This was her favourite brand!'

'Does this t-shirt come in any other colours?'

'He likes light blue!'

'Do you have this in medium?'

'She told me in a dream last night that she needs
me to buy her some herbal supplements!'

Were I only to hear the conversation, without knowing that the scene was a paper offering shop, I would imagine them to be a customer and a salesperson in a regular store. How else is one to know that the 'he' or 'she' they were speaking of had already left this world? These interactions show that the paper offerings shop and its offerings act as a bridge between the departed and their living relatives. While customers are buying paper offerings, it feels to them as if their ancestors are still here. And when they burn their offerings, they believe that their heartfelt wishes will be delivered across worlds to their ancestors.

常不經意聽到他們和老闆的談話：「這款手機有新型號嗎？這是他／她（生前）最愛用的牌子！」「這T恤有其他顏色嗎？他／她喜歡淺藍色呀！」「這有中碼嗎？」「他／她昨晚跟我報夢，著我替他／她買些補品呢！」如果只聽到對話而不知道場景是紙紮鋪，還以為這是在一般百貨店，顧客和店員的對話呢！豈會料到，顧客口中的他／她，早已遠走「他方」了。從這方面，我們可以體會到紙紮鋪及紙品，像是逝去者和親屬之間的橋梁，顧客在選購過程中，彷彿先人仍在，透過「化寶」（將紙品燒掉的意思），顧客相信先人會在另一時空收到他們的心意。

這些情景，往往使我想到我們祭祀文化中有個說法：「事死如事生！」所以孝子賢孫選購衣紙，一點也不馬虎。另外，顧客和紙紮鋪老闆的一問一答中，說不定還有紓緩生者對逝者思念的效用呢！這樣說來，紙品的功能是雙向的，它們不單是為逝者而設，對生者也有重大意義呢！

教學之餘，不知不覺，愛上泥塑。2000年我在上環一間畫廊舉辦陶塑個展「十台八里地誌之盂蘭勝會」，[2] 當時畫廊附近的皇后大道西有多間大型紙紮香燭鋪，裝置作品期間，我常在該區找尋些和展覽有關的配件。那些紙紮鋪相比起紅磡小區內的更見規模，紙品類別更多。因左鄰右里都在銷售同類貨品，競爭甚大，故衣紙陳列擺放也很講究，齊整有序，易見易取，儼如百貨公司及超市般。貨品

Such scenes remind me of a saying that comes from our offerings culture: 'treat the dead as if they are still alive!' With this in mind, devout relatives are attentive and conscientious when buying paper offerings for ancestors. What's more, this back and forth between customer and shop owner may well help to ease feelings of loss and grief. In this way, paper offerings have a two-way function: they are not only for the dead, but also have great significance for the living.

On top of my teaching, I unwittingly fell in love with ceramic sculpture. In 2000, I held an exhibition of clay figures called *Terraces Topography: Yu Lan Festival*[1] at a gallery in Sheung Wan. At the time, there were a number of large paper offering shops near the gallery on Queens Road West. While I was installing the show, I often searched the neighbourhood for accessories related to the exhibition. Compared with the paper shops in Hung Hom, these were much bigger and had many more types of paper offerings. There was a lot of competition for customers among these offering shops, and so their displays were quite particular. They were neat and orderly, and easy to browse and select—just like a department store or a supermarket. The offerings were too many to count. They were as small as batteries and as large as yachts, aeroplanes, sports cars, casinos, racecourses and even garden estate towers. There was gold and silver jewellery, gold bars, and all kinds of gold watches, diamond rings and other luxury goods. And as soon as a new model of tablet or mobile phone came on the market, the paper replicas would follow. As I stepped into one of these large paper shops, I suddenly felt this truly was a recreation of a real world. One after another, our everyday consumer desires and patterns of consumption were recreated. It was like a mirror, not only reflecting daily needs in the next world, but also reflecting this world's material desires and consumer culture. Consider, as an example, the paper shoes I collected. There are many styles and types: boys and girls, mens

多不勝數，小至一粒電芯，大至遊艇、飛機、跑車、賭場、馬場、花園大廈、金銀珠寶、金條金磚及各式金錶鑽戒等奢侈品。另外，平板電腦或手機，外邊市場上一有新型號上場，製造商很快便跟上。我鑽進其中較大的紙紮店，忽然覺得這兒是一個真實「世界」的翻版，紙醉金迷、醉生夢死。我們平日的消費模式、消費慾望，一一在此重現。這裏猶如一面鏡子，除了反映我們在另一世界日常所需要之外，同時也反映了我們今世的物慾和消費文化。就以我收集了的紙鞋為例，款式類別繁多：男女童鞋、男女成人鞋、中式、西式、屐、人字拖、拖鞋、涼鞋、波鞋、平底鞋、高跟鞋、長短靴、便服鞋、晚裝鞋……表面肌理看來似草的、布的、牛皮的、鱷魚皮的……另有繡花、通花、鑲花、鑲扣的、變化多端的鞋墊和鞋底圖案……還有大量模仿著名時裝品牌的款式，每款均有多種顏色和質感效果：金屬色、珍珠色、反光、啞面和半光啞，千變萬化，令人咋舌！遇過最特別的一對是鞋底印上不同腳底按摩穴位，令我忍俊不禁！

　　我們在生時只有一雙腳，死後雙腳還在嗎？聽説人死後，軀殼沒有了，只餘靈魂飄飄。那麼，這些紙鞋真的能在來世派上用場嗎？源源不絕推出市場的紙鞋，正是時下過度消費，濫做濫買的最佳例子。我慢慢萌生借「紙」諷今的念頭，並開始有策略地收集紙鞋，作為創作／展覽之用。

and womens, casual and formal, Chinese and Western, and imitations of famous fashion labels. There are clogs, flip-flops, slippers, sandals, sports shoes, flats, high heels, and low and high-cut boots. They come with finishes that replicate grass, cloth, cowhide and crocodile leather. There are shoes with floral embroidery, open weaves and decorative buckles. All these shoes come with a variety of insole and sole designs. And each style comes in several colours and with different textural effects: metallic, pearl, reflective, matte and semi-gloss. The endless permutations are amazing. The most unique pair I have encountered had the various points on the foot for reflexology massage printed on the soles—when I saw them, I couldn't help but smile.

2000 年「盂蘭勝會」展覽之後迄今，我一直以「靈魂之踭」（Soles for the Souls）系列來展示我的紙鞋收藏。我經常以裝置形式，模仿售賣皮鞋的陳列方法來展出它們——有時像間鞋店、有時像個櫥窗、有時像地攤。除了在香港，也曾帶它們去過澳洲布里斯班和日本東京展出。

2015 年德國學者沃爾夫岡・謝珀（Wolfgang Scheppe）將我當時收藏的 600 對紙鞋其中的 270 對，在他策展的「我的慾望」中展出。[3] 他直接從中國採購了兩個貨櫃的紙品，展出場地德國德勒斯登王宮搖身一變，成為一間比 Costco 還要大的超級百貨市場。他把紙品和全球化消費主義掛勾的概念，將我心目中，透過紙品來呈現超製、超賣和超買狀況的想法，推到極致。此外，展覽中最深印像的地方是，策展人將全部紙鞋，女先男後，以一直線排列，一對接一對，每對相隔一標準距離，貫穿展場 210 米的長度，我看到象徵無窮無盡，永無止境的慾望，十分震憾。誰的慾望？我的慾望！[4]

這也是我創作「靈魂之踭」展覽系列最吊詭的地方。我由批判過度消費開始，最後卻自投羅網，作繭自縛，不能自拔。工餘時我都在四出找尋不同款式的紙鞋，作為展覽之用。紙鞋猶如時裝，款式雖不至於有春夏秋冬四季更替，但每年清明及重陽時節，新鞋湧現，尤以清明為甚；故每年清明節前後，我都買個不亦樂乎，真是始料不及！

Above: Purpose-made 'gift packs' bought from the offering store
Right: D.I.Y. offerings made by the author from leftover packaging

We are born with a pair of feet, but will they still be there after we die? It is said that when we pass away the body is gone and only the floating soul remains. What use then do footless floating souls have for a pair of shoes? Surely the endless stream of paper shoes for the afterlife coming on the market must be the best example of contemporary over-consumption. Gradually, I developed the idea of using paper to satirise the present, and began strategically collecting paper shoes for my creative and curatorial purposes.

Since the Yu Lan Festival exhibition in 2000, I have been showing my paper shoe collection as the *Soles for the Souls* series. When I exhibit them, I often imitate the displays used to sell shoes—sometimes as a shoe store, sometimes as a window display,

上：作者利用剩餘包裝自製而成的祭品
左：購自紙紮店的特製「禮物包」

　　正如上文曾提及，不少紙鞋設計，都是透過電腦素描
和挪移手法，移形換影而成。由於過度像真，曾有著名時
裝品牌入稟法院，控告紙紮店出售侵權商品。由此可見，
紙品生產發行，亦可引起侵權及翻版糾紛，大可作為研究
知識產權的對象。

　　由收集紙鞋那天開始，我很少再購買其他紙品了，但
不等於我對它們失卻興趣。我一直留意它們的發展，廿多
年來，紙品包裝方面，早已形成一個模式，大部分有關日

sometimes as a street stall. As well as being shown in Hong Kong, the series has also been exhibited in Brisbane and Tokyo.

In 2015, German scholar Wolfgang Scheppe included 270 of the then six hundred shoes in my collection in his curatorial project *Supermarket of the Dead*.[2] For the exhibition, he purchased two shipping containers of paper offerings directly from China, transforming the Royal Palace in Dresden into a 'supermarket' that was bigger than a Costco. His concept, linking Chinese paper offerings with global consumerism, took my idea of showing overproduction and overconsumption through paper offerings to the extreme. The most striking image in the exhibition was the curator's arrangement of all the paper shoes in a straight line, womens followed by mens, one pair after another. The pairs were equally spaced through the exhibition hall in a straight line over 210 metres long. I was shocked to see this image of endless desire. And whose desire? My desire![3]

This was the most paradoxical aspect of the *Soles for the Souls* series. I started by criticising overconsumption, but in the end I fell into the trap myself and couldn't get out. I spent all my spare time looking everywhere for different styles of paper shoes to use in my exhibitions. Paper shoes are like fashion, however the styles do not change with the usual four seasons. Rather, each year at Ching Ming, and to a lesser extent the Double Ninth festival, a bounty of new styles appears.

As I mentioned, many paper shoe designs are created by computer drawing and digital manipulation. The accuracy of the reproduction was such that a famous fashion brand once filed a lawsuit against the paper stores for selling infringing goods. The production and distribution of paper products can also give rise to infringement and piracy disputes. And so paper offerings can also be an object of research into intellectual property rights.

常生活的衣食用品，多以一扁身紙盒盛載，盒蓋是透明的，盒內的物品一目了然，儼如一盒禮物。一則掃墓時方便攜帶，二則亦有利於紙紮鋪陳列存倉之用。禮盒內有些是模仿實物的紙品，諸如化妝品、鬚後水和假牙等。更多的是印上食物名稱大小不一的空殼紙盒，和我們在超市購買回來的各款食用品的紙包盒裝無異。

近年我把自己用過的小型包裝紙盒留下，先分類，後放進另一些收集回來的扁型大盒子內，權充禮盒供品，驟眼看來和紙紮鋪的商品分別不大。我自製紙品的出發點是，與其將一些燙了薄膠膜，不宜回收的彩色紙盒子送到堆填區，倒不如將它們循環再用，設計成另一產品。從來紙品最大的意義便是使逝者能繼續享有生前的生活，所以把在生時用過的盒子留下，來世還可使用呀！說不定有些盒子還包含紀念價值，特別值得保留 —— 是個人的回憶和故事呢！這個 D.I.Y. 禮盒紙品的想法可行嗎？大概不會有紙紮鋪老闆支持我吧！

2015年我應香港文化博物館的邀請，參與「時間遊人」展覽，我把這批以商品包裝自製而成的紙紮禮盒供品，放進博物館「新界文物館」的模擬紙紮鋪內，與購買回來的商業紙品並列，天衣無縫，沒多少觀眾能分真偽，只吃驚怎麼超市常見、大家常用的貨品，來了這裏！可堪玩味的地方是，買回來的禮盒供品以假作真，我自製的則是以真作假。

Since that day I began collecting paper shoes, I've rarely bought other paper offerings. But that's not to say that I've lost interest in them; I have always kept an eye on their development. Over the past twenty years, the packaging of paper offerings has taken a standard form: various products for daily life are packaged together in a flat box. The lid is transparent so that contents are clear at a glance, like a gift box. These packages are not only convenient to carry when going to tend to the family grave but also well suited to display and storage in the paper offerings shop. Inside these gift boxes are paper replicas of various real life objects such as cosmetics, aftershave or dentures. What's more, the printed designs on these empty cartons are no different to those on the packaging for the things we buy for ourselves at the supermarket.

In recent years, I have been keeping a lot of my own used paper packaging. I first sort the cartons, then put them into larger flat boxes that I've collected, so as to make 'gift packs' of offerings. At first glance, they are not so different from the products for sale at the paper offering shops. My motive for making these homemade paper offerings was that, rather than sending these colourful, non-recyclable laminated boxes to landfill, I might as well make them into a new product. The fundamental meaning of paper offerings has always been to allow the deceased to continue to enjoy the life they led before death. So why not save the boxes used in this life for use in the next? Perhaps some boxes may still hold value as keepsakes and might be worth holding on to for their personal memories and stories. Is my D.I.Y. paper offering gift box idea feasible? It's unlikely that the bosses of paper offering shops will get behind it!

In 2015, I was invited by the Hong Kong Heritage Hall to participate in the exhibition *Time Traveller*. I set up a replica paper offerings shop in the museum's New Territories Cultural Centre to display my homemade offering packs side by side with actual packs that I had

寫到這裏，也差不多了。對我來說，紙品的作用是多元的，既可化寶，又可展覽；既是另類設計，又是研究消費和翻版文化的材料；既是傳統工藝的延伸，又是祭祀文化的發展；既供逝者使用，又能同時安慰生者⋯⋯點只衣紙咁簡單！

1.　衣紙又可稱為紙品、紙紮、紙紮供品或紙紮貢品。

2.　「盂蘭節」—— 每年農曆七月七日是鬼節，港九有些街坊會或聯誼會發起主辦「盂蘭勝會」，設壇祭鬼並招渡亡魂。其中必須具備一大堆比真人還要高大兩、三倍的巨型紮作人偶，包括鬼王、判官、無常、鬼差、兵卒和馬匹等。還有海量的紙製金銀財帛及寶箱衣食等。這些都會在節後全部燒掉。「十台八里地誌之盂蘭勝會」乃香港理工大學設計學院支助研究。

3.　展覽資料請參閱《冥間超市》展覽目錄第一至三冊。Wolfgang Scheppe ed., *Supermarket of the Dead: Burnt Offerings in China and the Cult of Globalised Consumption*, Three volumes (Cologne: Verlag der Buchhandlung Walther Konig, 2015).

4.　Wolfgang Scheppe, ed., *Supermarket of the Dead: Burnt Offerings in China and the Cult of Globalised Consumption*. Vol. I *Zhizha Paper Shoes* (Cologne: Verlag der Buchhandlung Walther König, 2015). 2017 年 Wolfgang Scheppe 將部分紙鞋移師瑞士蘇黎世的約翰‧雅各布斯博物館 （Johann Jacobs Museum） 展出，展題為：*Holy Goods*。

bought from the paper offerings store. The effect was seamless. Few visitors noticed the difference—they only wondered how the familiar products from the supermarket shelf had ended up there! The interesting thing is that the gift boxes that I bought from the paper offering store were imitations pretending to be real, while the gift packs I made were real items pretending to be imitations.

And so, from my perspective, paper offerings play many roles. They can be burned for loved ones and they can be exhibited in a gallery. They are an unconventional kind of design, as well as a material for studying consumption and a reflection of knock-off culture. They are an extension of traditional crafts and a development of Chinese sacrificial culture. They are everyday comforts for the deceased, and at the same time, they give comfort to the living. Indeed, paper offerings have so much to offer.

1. Yu Lan festival, or Ghost Festival, is held each year on the seventh of July according to the lunar calendar. Some neighbourhoods or associations on Hong Kong Island and in Kowloon hold Yu Lan Fêtes, setting up altars for worshipping ghosts and beckoning dead souls. As part of the ritual, there must be a large number of giant puppets that are two or three times taller than real people. Among them are ghost kings, judges, ghost chasers, soldiers, and horses. There are also endless amounts of paper gold, silver, silk, treasure boxes and paper food and clothing, which are all burned after the festival. *Terraces Topography: Yu Lan Festival*, was an art exhibition presented by Rosanna Li at Para/Site Art Space, 31 Jan–12 Feb 2000. (Part of a research project funded by the Hong Kong Polytechnic University School of Design.)

2. Wolfgang Scheppe, ed., *Supermarket of the Dead: Burnt offerings in China and the cult of globalized consumption.* Vol. I *Zhizha Paper Shoes* (Cologne: Verlag der Buchhandlung Walther König, 2015).

3. In 2017, Wolfgang Scheppe moved some paper shoes to the Johann Jacobs Museum in Zurich, Switzerland, for the exhibition *Holy Goods*.

詞彙表 Glossary

英文 English	漢字 Chinese script	廣東話 Cantonese	普通話 Mandarin
ask rice woman	問米婆	man⁶mai⁵po⁴	wènmǐpó
Canton / Guangdong	廣東	Gwong²dung¹	Guǎngdōng
cheongsam	長衫	coeng⁴saam¹	chángshān
Ching Ming Festival	清明節	Cing¹ming⁴zit³	Qīngmíng jié
dim sum	點心	dim²sam¹	diǎn xin
Teochew / Chaozhou city	潮州	Ciu⁴zau¹	Cháozhōu
Double Ninth Festival	重陽節	Cung⁴joeng⁴zit³	Chóngyáng jié
Hong Kong style egg puff	雞蛋仔	gai¹daan⁶zai²	jīdànzǐ
Hungry Ghost Festival	鬼節	Gwai²zit³	Guǐ jié
mahjong	麻雀（麻將）	maa⁴zoek³	(májiāng)
oolong tea	烏龍茶	wu¹lung²caa⁴	wūlóng chá
ping on bun / peace bun	平安包	ping⁴on¹baau¹	píng'ān bāo
poon choi	盆菜	pun⁴coi³	pén cài
pu'erh tea / pu'er tea	普洱茶	pou²nei²caa⁴	pǔ'ěr chá
renminbi	人民幣	jan⁴man⁴bai⁶	rénmínbì
siu lung baau / xiao long bao	小籠包	siu²lung⁴baau¹	xiǎolóngbāo
siu maai / shaomai	燒賣	siu¹maai⁶	shāomài
siu mei (Cantonese barbeque)	燒味	siu¹mei⁶	shāowèi
Yuk Wong (Jade Emperor)	玉皇	Juk⁶Wong⁴	Yùhuáng
Yu Lan Festival	盂蘭節	Jyu⁴laan⁴zit³	Yúlán jié

Underworld Product and Service Providers

Banking and Financial Services

Heaven and Earth Bank of Clearance
p. 66, 67

Underworld Bank p. 68

Bank of Heaven and Earth p. 69

Bank of Hades (Heaven Main Office) p. 70

The Bank of Hell p. 71, 72, 73, 74, 75

Underworld Capital Bank p. 76

Transportation

Mingfu Airlines p. 62

Underworld Shipping Company p. 63

Underworld Rail Transport Company p. 64

Underworld Coach Transport Company p. 65

Food and Beverages

Underworld Tea Group, Ltd p. 98, 99

Excellent Tea Group, Ltd p. 99

'Hell-Known Brand' Dim Sum
Seafood Restaurant Premium Products p. 111

Underworld Food Conglomorate, Ltd p. 126, 127

Underworld Beverage Group p. 128

Underworld Beverage Products Ltd p. 128

Underworld Brewing Company, Ltd p. 129

Health and Pharmaceuticals

Underworld Drug Administration
p. 151, 152

King of Hell (Underworld)
Pharmaceutical Company, Ltd p. 149, 154

Underworld Pharmaceutical
Company, Ltd p. 144, 145, 148, 156

Fashion and Beauty

Underworld Clothing p. 46, 48

Underworld Cosmetics Company,
Ltd p. 135

Everyday needs

Underworld Tobacco Company p. 53

Underworld Daily Necessities
Company p. 132, 133

Superior Stationery Factory p. 171

Underworld Battery Company, Ltd p. 172

Culture and Entertainment

Underworld Mahjong House p. 158

Hades Opera Troupe p. 177

冥府產品和服務供應商

銀行和與融服務

天地通銀行有限公司
頁 66、67、74

冥府銀行 頁 68、75

天地銀行 頁 69

地府銀行（冥國總行）頁 70

冥通銀行 頁 71、72、73

冥都銀行 頁 76

交通運輸

冥府航空集團公司 頁 62

冥府輪船運輸公司 頁 63

冥府火車運輸公司 頁 64

冥府汽車運輸公司 頁 65

飲食

冥府茶業集團有限公司 頁 98、99

優佳茶業有限公司 頁 99

「冥牌」海鮮酒樓點心精品 頁 111

冥府食品集團有限公司 頁 126、127

冥府飲品集團 頁 128

冥府飲料制品有限公司 頁 128

冥府啤酒制品有限公司 頁 129

健康與製藥

冥府藥品監督局 頁 151、152

閻羅王（冥府）藥業有限公司
頁 149、154

冥府藥業有限公司
頁 144、145、148、156

時尚與美容

冥府服裝 頁 46、48

冥都化妝品有限公司 頁 135

日常需求

冥府煙草公司 頁 53

冥府日用品公司 頁 132、133

優佳文具廠 頁 171

冥都電池有限公司 頁 172

文化娛樂

冥府雀館 頁 158

冥都劇團 頁 177

照片索引　Index of Photographs

38　眼鏡和眼鏡盒
Glasses with case

39　染色眼鏡和眼鏡盒
Tinted glasses with case

40　花呢格子襯裏高跟皮靴
Leather boots with
tartan lining

41　長衫（旗袍）
Cheongsam

42　拉鍊手袋
Handbag with functional zip

43　高跟鞋
High-heeled shoes

44　拖鞋
Slippers

45　功夫鞋
Kungfu style slippers

46　金色西裝
Gold suit

47　金錶
Gold watch

48　冷衫
Cardigan

49　馬球衫
Polo shirt

50　拉鍊外套
Jacket with functional zip

51　拉鍊羽絨外套
Down jacket with
functional zip

52　男裝配飾
Gentleman's accessories

53　香煙
Cigarettes

54　收摺的雨傘
Umbrella (down)

55　撐開的雨傘
Umbrella (up)

56　護照（封面）
Passport (cover)

57　護照（內頁）
Passport (inside)

58　回鄉證（舊版，封面）
Home return permit
(old format, cover)

59　回鄉證（舊版，內頁）
Home return permit
(old format, inside)

60　回鄉證（現行版）
Home return permit
(current format)

61 八達通
Octopus card

62 機票及行李認領證
Airline ticket and
baggage check

63 船票
Passenger ship ticket

64 火車票
Railway ticket

65 大巴客票
Coach ticket

66 冥鈔（港幣 20 元）
Banknote (20 HKD)

67 冥鈔（港幣 100 元）
Banknote (100 HKD)

68 冥鈔（港幣 500 元）
Banknote (500 HKD)

69 冥鈔（港幣 1,000 元）
Banknote (1,000 HKD)

70 支票簿
Chequebook

71 支票
Cheque

72 銀行存摺（封面）
Bank passbook (closed)

73 銀行存摺（內頁）
Bank passbook (open)

74 銀行卡
Bank card

75 金條套裝
Gold bars

76 金條
Gold bar

77 手槍
Handgun

78 電筒
Torch

79 望遠鏡
Binoculars

80 冷氣機（窗口式）
Air conditioner (window unit)

81 掛鐘
Wall clock

82 洗衣機
Washing machine

83 雪櫃
Refrigerator

84 熨斗
Clothes iron

85 風筒
Hair dryer

86 座枱風扇，扇葉、鎖頭（朝左）
Desk Fan with rotating blades
and head (facing left)

87 座枱風扇，扇葉、鎖頭（朝右）
Desk fan with rotating blades
and head (facing right)

88 斑點狗
Dalmatian

89 棕色狗
Brown dog

90 狗糧
Dog treats

91 寵物背心
Vest for a pet

92 竹鳥籠和了哥
Bamboo bird cage
with songbird

93 暖水壺
Vacuum flask

94 茶葉罌
Tea caddy

95 藥煲和爐
Medicine pot and stove

96 茶壺
Teapot

97 茶杯
Tea cups

98 鐵觀音烏龍茶
Iron Goddess oolong tea

99 普洱茶
Pu'erh tea

100 電飯煲
Rice cooker

101 搪瓷碗與匙羹
Enamelled bowl and spoon

102 火龍果
Dragon fruit

103 水果拼盤
Assorted fruits

104 鳳爪
Chicken feet

105 蒸餃餃子
Steamed dumplings

106 燒賣
Siu maai (dumplings)

107 小籠包
Siu lung baau
(steamed soup dumplings)

108 茶果，綠色
Glutinous rice cake (green)

109 茶果，白色
Glutinous rice cake (white)

110 蛋糕
Cakes

111 芒果班戟
Mango pancakes

112 蒸餛飩
Steamed wontons

113 炸餛飩
Fried wontons

114 龍蝦
Lobster

115 魚翅
Shark fin

116 燒味飯
Siu mei (roast meat) with rice

117 壽司拼盤
Sushi platter

118 甜品拼盤
Assorted desserts

119 冰皮月餅
Snow-skin style mooncakes

120 蛋撻
Egg tarts

121 蛋捲
Egg rolls

122 雞蛋仔
Gai daan zai
(Hong Kong style egg puffs)

123 銅鑼燒
Dorayaki (Japanese pancake)

124 馬卡龍
Macarons

125 平安包
Ping on (peace) bun

126 檸檬茶
Lemon iced tea

127 咖啡
Coffee

128 啤酒
Beer

129 啤酒
Beer

130 牙膏
Toothpaste

131 牙膏
Toothpaste

132 牙膏
Toothpaste

133 漱口水
Mouthwash

134 剃鬚刀和刀片
Razor with cartridges

135 男士專用剃鬚膏
Men's shaving cream

136 假牙清潔錠
Denture cleanser

137 假牙
Denture

138 助聽器
Hearing aid

139 輪椅
Wheelchair

140 潤喉薄荷糖
Mint

141 薄荷膏
Menthol ointment

142 萬金油（正面）
Heat balm (front)

143 萬金油（頂）
Heat balm (top)

144 活絡油
Wood lock liniment
(herbal ointment for pain relief)

145 枇杷膏
Loquat syrup
(traditional sore throat remedy)

146 保嬰丹
Bo Ying compound
(traditional remedy for
soothing infant discomfort)

147 膠布
Sticking plaster

148 止痛露
Analgesic liquid

149 驅風油
Medicated menthol oil

150 外敷藥油
Medicated topical oil

151 木餾油丸（腸胃藥）
Creosote digestive pills

152 止咳丸
Cough pills

153 追風油
Topical pain relieving oil

154 止咳丸
Cough pill

155 鎮痛藥布
Analgesic sticking plaster

156 止痕藥膏
Itch lotion
(for insect bites and rashes)

157 人參
Ginseng

158 麻雀套裝
Mahjong set

159 象棋
Chinese chess set

160 乒乓球拍
Ping pong bat

161 乒乓球與球拍
Ping pong ball and bat

162 足球
Football

163 溜冰鞋
Rollerskates

164 掌上遊戲機及觸控筆
Handheld game console with stylus

165 掌上遊戲機
Handheld game console

166 電單車
Motorbike

167 綿羊仔
Scooter

168 攝影機
Video camera

169 小型攝影機
Camcorder

170 袖珍計算機
Pocket calculator

171 擦膠
Eraser

172 電芯（AA型）
Batteries (AA type)

173 記憶卡
Memory card

174 智能手機
Smartphone

175 音樂播放器
Music player

176 隨身聽（AM/FM電台收音機）
Walkman with AM/FM radio

177 卡式錄音帶 ——《帝女花》
Compact cassette—Cantonese
opera (Princess Chang Ping)

178 附薦袋上的花卉圖案
Floral motif from a bag for
burning paper offerings

高峰，視覺設計師、作家和策展人。生於澳洲，在澳洲悉尼科技大學修讀視覺傳達設計與國際研究，並曾在昆明雲南師範大學與台南國立成功大學學習中文。他對東亞文化特別感興趣，過去 15 年間曾於日本、香港、台灣和中國內地工作和生活。除了從事視覺設計和策劃展覽外，他同時任教於悉尼科技大學設計學院，教授和寫作有關物質文化與設計，曾帶領學生到香港進行文化交流。

Chris Gaul is a visual designer, writer and curator who takes a particular interest in the material culture of East Asia. He was born in Australia and over the past fifteen years has lived and worked in Japan, Hong Kong, Taiwan and Mainland China. He studied Design and International Studies at the University of Technology and Chinese language and culture at Yunnan Normal University in Kunming and National Cheng Kung University in Tainan. In addition to working as a visual designer, he teaches at the UTS School of Design, curates exhibitions and writes and lectures on material culture and design.

DESIGNTRUST
信言設計大使
AN INITIATIVE OF THE
HONG KONG AMBASSADORS
OF DESIGN

該計劃獲得信言設計大使的支持。信言設計大
使只對計劃提供資助，除此以外並不會參與在
計劃當中。上述出版（或計劃團隊成員）所表
達的任何意見、發現、結論或建議，僅代表計
劃團隊，並不反映信言設計大使的立場。

This project has received support from Design
Trust. Design Trust has provided funding support
only and has not otherwise taken part in the
project. Any opinions, findings, conclusions or
recommendations expressed in this publication
are those of the authors only and do not reflect
the views of Design Trust.